HOW TO GROW AND USE
ANNUALS

A Sunset Book

By the editorial staffs of
Sunset Books and Sunset Magazine

LANE BOOK COMPANY
MENLO PARK, CALIFORNIA

FOREWORD

ANNUALS ARE WONDERFUL. They bring maximum color to a garden in minimum time—in every color imaginable. Most of them are inexpensive. They come in all shapes and sizes. No plants are easier to grow. They provide an element of fun and a sense of discovery for any gardener—from the fumbling beginner to the experienced plantsman.

Perhaps the most noteworthy quality of annuals is their ability to grow in a hurry; they are the speed merchants of the gardening world. Several dozen petunia seeds—to the human eye, almost undistinguishable from grains of pepper—can develop into a mass of gay color and lush foliage in just a few months. Zinnia seeds, larger and easier to handle, are even faster —bringing summer-long color to your garden in as little as six weeks. If this is not fast enough for you, purchase some young plants at a nursery; some kinds are available in full bloom, and many others require only a few days or weeks after transplanting to begin their flowering season.

Annuals are especially effective as problem-solvers. Spot a few here and there as fillers in bare spots and corners, between young shrubs, or among perennials. Try them as edgings, background plantings, or bulb covers. If you have the space and the proper situation, mass them in one or two locations. Above all, let this be your rule: Put them where you can see them and enjoy their color to the fullest.

Much of the material in this book originated in the garden pages of *Sunset,* the Magazine of Western Living. For many years, *Sunset Magazine* and its publishing counterpart, *Sunset Books,* have been the recognized authorities on gardening (as well as many other subjects) to green-thumbers throughout the verdant, fertile gardening country of the West. *The Sunset Western Garden Book* is so widely accepted as the ultimate authority on gardening that many nurseries keep well-thumbed copies of the book on their counters so that customers and employes alike may refer to it.

How to Grow and Use Annuals, like many other *Sunset Books,* was written and edited for gardeners throughout the country. In compiling material on annuals, *Sunset's* garden editors pooled their own first-hand knowledge with cultural information from seedsmen and plantsmen in every section of the United States. We at Sunset extend our sincere thanks to these experts in the field, without whose generous cooperation this book would not have been possible.

Many of the photographs on these pages, including some of those in color, were donated by the Ferry-Morse Seed Company. For this, also, we are indeed grateful.

Eighth Printing May 1970

COLOR PAGES BY SWEENEY, KRIST AND DIMM, PORTLAND, OREGON

CONTENTS

On the cover:

Marigold varieties are: yellow double— 'Toreador' (All-America); large orange double—Miracle hybrids; rusty red—'Fandango'; small orange flowers—'Spun Gold' (All-America). The photograph is by Ernest Braun.

Title page

The long, graceful flowers on the title page are Bells of Ireland, renowned everywhere as one of the greatest cutting flowers. The photographer was Jeannette Grossman.

WHAT ARE ANNUALS?

ANNUALS are plants whose life cycle is completed in a single season—the seed germinates, the plant grows, blooms, sets seed, and dies. In almost every case growth is rapid, and this is why gardeners all over the world look to annuals for quick color.

Some annuals, such as zinnias and sweet alyssum, rush from seed to flower in less than 2 months. Transplants, available by the dozen or in flats at nurseries, often begin to bloom a few weeks after planting—some may even be about ready to bloom when you buy them.

Biennials—Treat Them as Annuals

Biennials are similar to annuals in many ways—so much so, in fact, that you will find a good many of them in this book, since they are treated in much the same way as annuals.

Actually, biennials occupy a halfway position between annuals and perennials. Like perennials, they take two growing seasons to reach the blooming period; however, like annuals, most of them flower but once, then die. (Some biennials, such as hollyhock and foxglove, re-seed themselves so readily you have a new supply of plants each year.) Generally speaking, biennials bloom earlier in the year than most annuals; spring and early summer are usually their peak flowering seasons.

If you live in a mild climate, the best time to sow biennials is between June and August. By fall, the seedlings will be large enough to transplant to the garden. If you do not wish to be bothered with caring for small plants during the summer months, or if you live in a cold climate where it is not practical to plant them out in the fall, it is best to sow seed in August, keep the seedlings in flats or pots in a coldframe, and set the plants out in spring.

How to Use Annuals

Even the smallest garden has room for some annuals, even if nothing more than a few pots of marigolds or lobelia. Today's trend toward low maintenance gardens with all their paving, gravel, or ground covers doesn't eliminate the need for annuals. In fact, the garden largely given over to paving and structure often needs their color most, and its very design frequently lends itself to some dramatic displays of concentrated color. The raised bed is an ideal staging area, and so are the many pockets left under trees or around a paved patio. And, of course, you can also grow annuals in pots or in some of the interesting ceramic, concrete, wood, and other kinds of containers now available. It's only a matter of choosing annuals that are in proper scale, and adapted to the exposure.

With annuals alone you can have a succession of bloom throughout the year in warm winter sections, and from before last frost in the spring to beyond first frost in the fall in the cold winter areas. But succession of bloom requires planning and close attention to planting dates. Many gardeners, planning for spring, summer, and winter flowers, haven't the heart to pull out and replace the spring blooming crop in time to get the summer crop under way.

For many gardeners, the most satisfactory way to use annuals is in combination with perennials and shrubs. When a garden is not entirely dependent upon annuals, the bringing in of seasonal color seems to be an easy task. But when the garden is so arranged that it falls apart unless every flower is in full dress, the planting and care of annuals may become a chore.

Types and Varieties

Much of the fun and success you will have with annuals depends on how well you know the varieties and kinds available. Some of the most popular (marigolds, zinnias, and petunias, to name a few) come in so many different varieties, sizes, colors, and forms, that growing any one of these annuals can make a fascinating hobby for the gardener who likes to specialize.

We have suggested certain varieties of each annual in this book so that the reader will have some sort of starting point when he goes out to scan the seed racks or browse through the nursery. There are, of course, hundreds of other excellent varieties, but it would be impossible to mention all of them here. (Most seed companies will send you, on request, a free catalog.)

One way to be sure you are getting proven varieties is to look for the "All-America Selections" emblem on the seed packets and in catalogs. This program, first started in 1932, is sponsored by several seedsmen's organizations in order to test and evaluate new flower and vegetable introductions in trial grounds in various climates of the United States.

To ask a commercial flower hybridizer what he's working on and what he plans to offer the home gardener next year is like asking one of the automobile companies to show you a photograph of next year's model. Flower hybridizing is a highly competitive business, and new introductions take years of intensive technical work and much patience before they ever make their appearance on the seed racks.

Although we can't forecast exactly what new flowers you'll be buying in years to come, you can anticipate a greater refining of many of the more popular flowers—better colors, more resistance to heat and disease, earlier blooms in some varieties, compact growth habit, and more freely blooming flowers. And, of course, there will be some real novelties coming along, perhaps a blue zinnia or a clear white marigold.

AVERAGE HARD-FROST DATES*

Based on U.S.D.A. weather records

State	Last in Spring	First in Fall	State	Last in Spring	First in Fall	State	Last in Spring	First in Fall
Alabama, N. W.	Mar. 25	Oct. 30	Kentucky	Apr. 15	Oct. 20	N. Dakota, E.	May 16	Sept. 20
Alabama, S. E.	Mar. 8	Nov. 15	Louisiana, No.	Mar. 13	Nov. 10	Ohio, No.	May 6	Oct. 15
Arizona, No.	Apr. 23	Oct. 19	Louisiana, So.	Feb. 20	Nov. 20	Ohio, So.	Apr. 20	Oct. 20
Arizona, So.	Mar. 1	Dec. 1	Maine	May 25	Sept. 25	Oklahoma	Apr. 2	Nov. 2
Arkansas, No.	Apr. 7	Oct. 23	Maryland	Apr. 19	Oct. 20	Oregon, W.	Apr. 17	Oct. 25
Arkansas, So.	Mar. 25	Nov. 3	Massachusetts	Apr. 25	Oct. 25	Oregon, E.	June 4	Sept. 22
California			Michigan, Upper Pen.	May 25	Sept. 15	Pennsylvania, W.	Apr. 20	Oct. 10
Imperial Valley	Jan. 25	Dec. 15	Michigan, No.	May 17	Sept. 25	Pennsylvania, Cen.	May 1	Oct. 15
Interior Valley	Mar. 1	Nov. 15	Michigan, So.	May 10	Oct. 8	Pennsylvania, E.	Apr. 17	Oct. 15
Southern Coast	Jan. 15	Dec. 15	Minnesota, No.	May 25	Sept. 15	Rhode Island	Apr. 25	Oct. 25
Central Coast	Feb. 25	Dec. 1	Minnesota, So.	May 11	Oct. 1	S. Carolina, N. W.	Apr. 1	Nov. 8
Mountain Sections	Apr. 25	Sept. 1	Mississippi, No.	Mar. 25	Oct. 30	S. Carolina, S. E.	Mar. 15	Nov. 15
Colorado, West	May 25	Sept. 18	Mississippi, So.	Mar. 15	Nov. 15	S. Dakota	May 15	Sept. 25
Colorado, N. E.	May 11	Sept. 27	Missouri	Apr. 20	Oct. 20	Tennessee	Apr. 10	Oct. 25
Colorado, S. E.	May 1	Oct. 15	Montana	May 21	Sept. 22	Texas, N. W.	Apr. 15	Nov. 1
Connecticut	Apr. 25	Oct. 20	Nebraska, W.	May 11	Oct. 4	Texas, N. E.	Mar. 21	Nov. 10
Delaware	Apr. 15	Oct. 25	Nebraska, E.	Apr. 15	Oct. 15	Texas, So.	Feb. 10	Dec. 15
District of Columbia	Apr. 11	Oct. 23	Nevada, W.	May 19	Sept. 22	Utah	Apr. 26	Oct. 19
Florida, No.	Feb. 25	Dec. 5	Nevada, E.	June 1	Sept. 14	Vermont	May 23	Sept. 25
Florida, Cen.	Feb. 11	Dec. 28	New Hampshire	May 23	Sept. 25	Virginia, No.	Apr. 15	Oct. 25
Florida, South of Lake Okeechobee, almost frost-free			New Jersey	Apr. 20	Oct. 25	Virginia, So.	Apr. 10	Oct. 30
Georgia, No.	Apr. 1	Nov. 1	New Mexico, No.	Apr. 23	Oct. 17	Washington, W.	Apr. 10	Nov. 15
Georgia, So.	Mar. 15	Nov. 15	New Mexico, So.	Apr. 1	Nov. 1	Washington, E.	May 15	Oct. 1
Idaho	May 21	Sept. 22	New York, W.	May 10	Oct. 8	W. Virginia, W.	May 1	Oct. 15
Illinois, No.	May 1	Oct. 8	New York, E.	May 1	Oct. 15	W. Virginia, E.	May 15	Oct. 1
Illinois, So.	Apr. 15	Oct. 20	New York, No.	May 15	Oct. 1	Wisconsin, No.	May 17	Sept. 25
Indiana, No.	May 1	Oct. 8	N. Carolina, W.	Apr. 15	Oct. 25	Wisconsin, So.	May 1	Oct. 10
Indiana, So.	Apr. 15	Oct. 20	N. Carolina, E.	Apr. 8	Nov. 1	Wyoming, W.	June 20	Aug. 20
Iowa, No.	May 1	Oct. 2	N. Dakota. W.	May 21	Sept. 13	Wyoming, E.	May 21	Sept. 20
Iowa, So.	Apr. 15	Oct. 9						
Kansas	Apr. 20	Oct. 15						

*Allow 10 days either side of above dates to meet local conditions and seasonal differences.

HOW TO GROW ANNUALS

THE RULES for successful cultivation of annuals are few and simple, but it is important that they be taken seriously. Absolute "musts" are a carefully prepared, well-drained garden bed; a sunny location (there are exceptions); and sufficient water.

This chapter is a summation of general cultural techniques. For specific information about each annual, see the chapters beginning on pages 32 and 60.

The Magic of Seed Gardening

Growing your own plants from seed gives great satisfaction to most people who've tried it—including the child who pokes a few nasturtium seeds into the ground and is fascinated that anything happens, and the novice adult who seeds alyssum in a new garden just to cover raw ground and is amazed when almost every seed germinates.

This experience in gardening appeals to most people, but some may feel it's beyond them. They may have tried it at some time with sad results, or they may just be reluctant to try. How difficult is it?

Not many plants will perform well if you merely scatter a handful of seeds across a patch of sun-baked soil. A certain amount of preliminary work is necessary before you sow seed, and a fair amount of care after that. But these steps aren't difficult, and success isn't dependent on any magical powers you may think good gardeners possess. If you follow the steps below, you can't miss. You can sow your seeds in the open ground or start them in flats; there are advantages to each method. Either way, you will have one big advantage if you grow from seed: You will be able to grow some of the annuals that are not available in nursery flats.

You can vary the procedure described below a fair amount and still get good results.

Sowing Seed in Open Ground

Advantages. Plants grown from seed where they are to remain often flower sooner than flat-grown plants, for you do save some growing time by eliminating the shock of transplanting. Many growers feel that you not only get more plants for your money from a packet of seed sown in open ground, but that plants will be more vigorous and have a longer blooming period than plants of the same seed if started in flats.

When to sow. You gain nothing by sowing seed too early in cold and/or wet soil. Seed may rot, and the chances are you'll get spotty germination or stunted plants. In frost-free areas, open ground seeding can get underway in February. April and May are best in most other areas.

Soil preparation. If you know a home gardener who has had bad luck growing plants from seed, more than likely the failure can be traced to poor soil preparation. Stirring up the soil with a power cultivator usually is not enough; you have to get humus

into the soil. Spread 2 or 3 inches of peat moss, leaf mold, ground bark, rotted manure, or other humous material over the seed bed; also add superphosphate or bonemeal, about 3 to 5 pounds for 100 square feet. To heavy soils add gypsum or dolomite, about 10 to 15 pounds per 100 square feet.

Using a spade or a power cultivator, thoroughly mix these materials with the soil to a depth of 6 to 8 inches. Break clods with the back of a shovel. Rake and make level. Apply an all-purpose insecticide-fungicide to prevent insect attack and damping-off disease.

This may sound like a lot of work just to grow a few dozen annuals. However, once the soil is well prepared, it doesn't take much time or effort to keep it in good condition for successive plantings.

How to sow. On the back of the seed packet you'll find directions. You can sow in rows, or broadcast the

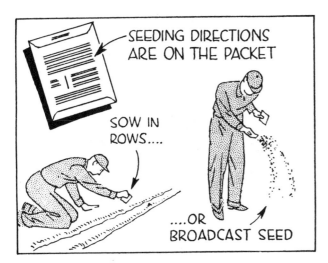

SEEDING DIRECTIONS ARE ON THE PACKET

SOW IN ROWS....

....OR BROADCAST SEED

seed. In either case, cover the seed with about ¼ inch of coarse sawdust or peat moss; then firm with the back of a rake.

Soak the seedbed with a fine mist sprayer. If you have to water by hand, adjust the nozzle to a fine spray, and go back and forth over the bed until the soil is well soaked. Don't use a strong jet of water or you'll disturb the seed and create puddles of water. Water again when the soil under the mulch looks dry. Try to anticipate drying-out by watering more often when weather is hot or windy.

When seed germinates. After seeds germinate (usually 7 to 10 days), cover with wire or plastic mesh (supported above the seedlings) for protection from birds. If snails or slugs are a problem in your area, set out bait.

Thinning out. After two pairs of true leaves develop, thin crowded plants by removal or transplanting. If you live in a cool-summer area, follow spacing instructions on the packet. In hot climates, close

IN HOT, DRY INLAND AREAS, PLANTS GROWN CLOSE TOGETHER HELP SHADE SOIL-KEEP IT COOL

IN COASTAL OR HUMID AREAS, THIN SEEDLINGS TO PREVENT MILDEW, ALLOW GROUND TO WARM UP

planting is a good idea; the plants shade the soil, thus helping to keep the roots cool and moist.

Feeding. The idea is to keep annuals growing fast. About 14 days after germination, feed with liquid fertilizer high in nitrogen. Feed every 2 weeks until flower buds form, then use a food low in nitrogen, high in phosphorus and potassium. Sprinkle overhead after feeding to wash fertilizer from the foliage, so that the leaves won't be burned.

Watering. Overhead watering is satisfactory until buds start to open; after blossoms unfold, flood irrigate whenever possible, or use a watering tube. Water again when the top inch of soil is dry.

Sowing Seed in Flats

Advantages. You can control the soil mix, you can move flats around so the plants get the right amount of sun or shade, watering is easier, and you notice pest damage quicker and take necessary steps before there is much loss. It's the best method to use for expensive or very fine seed, for seed that takes a long time to germinate, and for vegetables and hot weather annuals that you want to start early when the ground outside is still too cold or wet. To take full advantage of this method, you should have a greenhouse, coldframe, hotbed, or other sheltered place in which to protect seeded flats and (later) small transplants from inclement weather. Many gardeners, of course, start seeds in kitchen or basement windows, or on glass-enclosed, heated porches.

When to sow. You have to wait about 2½ to 4 months to get bloom from most annuals started from

PLAN AHEAD— IT TAKES FROM 2½ TO 4 MONTHS FOR MOST ANNUALS TO BLOOM FROM SEED

SEEDLINGS ARE READY TO SET OUT IN ABOUT 8 TO 10 WEEKS...

seed in April; this includes 8 to 10 weeks in the flat, from the time you sow the seed until the plants are ready to set out in the garden. You have to plan ahead. Get seed started as soon as possible; time your efforts so the plants are ready to set out at the right time. But it's not a good idea to hold them back by keeping them in the flat.

Soil preparation. Most gardeners have their own pet mixes, but the important thing is to use a mix that is loose, drains well (won't cake like clay), yet holds moisture. Equal parts of coarse river sand, leaf mold or peat moss, and garden loam make a good basic mix. Screen it through a ¼-inch mesh.

To prevent damping-off (a soil fungus that attacks seed and tiny seedlings), treat the seeding mixture with a commercial fungicide, or start the seed in a sterile medium such as sphagnum moss, vermiculite, or perlite. Rather than treat the entire seeding mixture, many gardeners treat the seeds themselves by pouring a small amount of the fungicide powder into the seed packet and shaking it to coat the seeds.

Containers to use. Flats are commonly used, but you can also use pots, boxes, or any other container that has drainage holes in the bottom. It all depends on how many seeds you want to start.

How to sow. Fill the container ½ to ¾ inch from the top with the seeding mix. Firm with a block of wood or the palm of your hand. Mark off rows with a ruler or piece of lath, pressing it ⅛ to ¼ inch deep into the mix (fine seeds need not be buried). A pencil also serves as a convenient tool for marking rows and lifting small seedlings for transplanting.

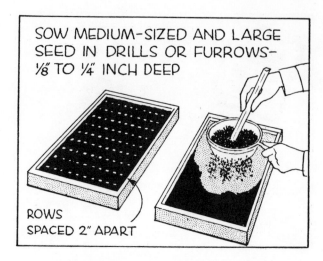

Water carefully with a fine mist to prevent disturbing the seed; many gardeners soak the seed container from below (in a sink or large basin)—the best method, particularly for very fine seed. Cover with wet newspaper and a pane of glass. Place the container in a warm spot, but not in direct sun. If you don't have a greenhouse or coldframe, a garage or back porch with some morning sun is a satisfactory substitute. Keep the seeding mixture moist, but not saturated, at all times. (If the soil mixture was thoroughly moistened at time of seeding, it may not be necessary—especially in the case of fast germinating seeds—to water until after the seedlings appear.) Lift the covering every day, starting about one week or less after seeding, to see whether the seeds have started to germinate.

When seed germinates. When growth starts, remove the covering and move the container into a brighter, more open location such as a lathhouse or under a high branching tree, but still not in full sun.

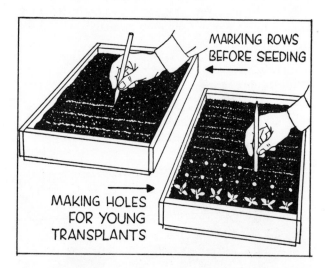

Space rows about 2 inches apart. Sow seeds in the little furrows and cover with sand, sifted peat moss, or sifted bark. Firm again so there's good contact between the seed and the mixture. Label clearly.

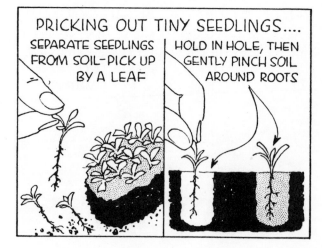

Pricking out. This term simply means lifting the tiny seedlings when they have two sets of true leaves and moving them into larger quarters where they have room to develop. First fill flats with a slightly richer mixture than the one in which you started the seed—a good one is 2 parts garden loam, 1 part river sand, and 1 part sifted peat moss or leaf mold. Then lift out small clumps of seedlings; separate them gently with fingers, or a pointed stick or pencil. Space seedlings about 1½ inches apart in holes made with the unsharpened end of the stick or pencil, and gently firm the soil around the roots. When the flat is filled, water in the seedlings, and place the flat in light shade for 2 or 3 days before moving it into half sun.

Keep the seedlings watered. Gradually expose them to more sun so that, by the time they are ready to set out in the garden (in 4 or 5 weeks—or when plants touch each other) they can take full sunlight without wilting.

Transplanting

Regardless of how successful you are at starting seeds and growing them on in flats, your efforts will go for nought unless you follow proper transplanting procedures. Here are some rules that will help you get your plants off to a good start.

Prepare beds before you plant. Throw out any large unbreakable clods. If the soil is sandy or heavy, work in rotted manure, peat moss, or other good humous materials. To enrich poor soil, scratch a complete commercial fertilizer (per label instructions) into the surface. Water soil down well at least a day before you plant, or fill each planting hole with water and let it soak in before planting.

Choose the right time of day. Cloudy or foggy days are ideal for setting out plants, preferably in early morning. Next best time is the late afternoon, for the plants then have the night hours in which to recover from the initial shock of transplanting. This is especially helpful to zinnias, marigolds, petunias, and other plants with large leaf surfaces.

Make good-sized planting holes. Dig generous-sized planting holes, cutting the sides vertically with the trowel instead of sloping them inward. Work up the soil in the bottom to make a soft cushion for the roots to penetrate.

Lift plants carefully. When you dig the small plants out of the flats, try to keep as much soil as possible around the roots. This is a lot easier to do if the soil is on the moist side. Try separating (blocking out) the plants and lifting them out with a spatula or putty knife; *do not* use a trowel.

Plant slightly low. (Stock is an exception—plant it slightly high.) Place the plant in the hole, slightly lower than it was in the flat; fill in around it with well pulverized, slightly moist soil, and leave a shallow basin around the transplant. Water it thoroughly.

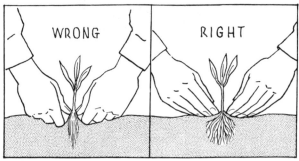

WRONG — DON'T SQUEEZE ROOTS

RIGHT — GENTLY FIRM IN

Mulch. To keep the ground from drying out rapidly, place a mulch of peat moss, ground bark, sawdust, or dry grass clippings around the plants.

Shade if necessary. If the weather is hot, shade the plants from direct sun for a few days with cardboard,

Make this portable shade for seedlings from laths nailed 1 inch apart on two 1 by 3's; set it on 10-inch stilts.

RICHARD DAWSON

shingles; or burlap, newspapers, or wrapping paper supported on stakes. A good-sized portable lath frame is the best solution of all. It is easy and inexpensive to make, will shade a number of plants simultaneously, stores easily, and can be pressed into service at a moment's notice. It can be used for many other garden jobs, such as providing part shade for flats of young seedlings.

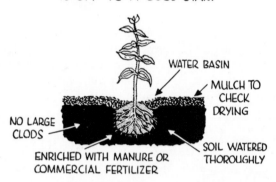

HERE IS AN ANNUAL THAT IS OFF TO A GOOD START

WATER BASIN

MULCH TO CHECK DRYING

NO LARGE CLODS

ENRICHED WITH MANURE OR COMMERCIAL FERTILIZER

SOIL WATERED THOROUGHLY

Buying Nursery Transplants

Even if you like seed gardening, it is likely that you will buy some of your annuals from nurseries. Rare is the gardener—especially on the first warm day of spring—who doesn't feel the impulse to take home a dozen of this-or-that as he strolls past row-on-row of young bedding plants.

If you are a nursery shopper, it is wise to know some of the basic rules for selecting the annuals capable of giving you the most for your money.

Look for full-foliaged, compact little plants. A well-branched small plant usually has a larger, stronger root system than a tall, leggy plant.

Foliage indicates a plant's health and vigor. Strong plants have leaves that feel crisp and are a fresh green, with no yellowing or browning at the edges. Drooping leaves may indicate weak plants grown without sufficient water, air, and light—or perhaps they were frost-nipped.

Though flats of plants already showing bloom are more tempting, pass them up for younger plants. Those in bloom soon fade, while the younger ones—even if they are budded—have a chance to adapt to your garden before flowers open and usually stay in bloom longer.

When buying seedlings by the dozen, see that they are removed from flats carefully, with soil around their roots. Feeder roots exposed to air will dry out, giving plants a crippling setback.

Commercial Refinements

Several products introduced in recent years might be called refinements on the age-old methods of growing plants from seed; products that make it easier for you. For example, there are seed or plant starters. All you do is remove the lid of the container (or punch holes in it), and water. Seed, humus, and nutrients may all be in the container, or the seed may be in a separate packet so you can sow it yourself. The seeding medium is sterile, so you don't have to worry about damping-off fungus.

If you want to grow some of the lesser known annuals that aren't put up in pre-seeded packages, or carried by bedding plant growers, then you'll be interested in the kits that come with small pots of plastic or some compressed material, a seeding mix, plant labels, and even a heating cable. Other kits contain the pots or liners, and a plastic tray or stand to hold them. The polyethylene wrapper can be used to cover the pots after seeding, to speed up germination.

Or you can just buy the small pots made of compressed peat moss, manure, or other material such as vermiculite. You fill them with good soil and put a seed or two (or a tiny seedling) in each one, then when the seedlings are large enough to transplant, you plant pot and all. Roots grow right through the walls of the pot, and the plants don't suffer any transplanting shock. You also don't lose any soil from around the roots, as so frequently happens when you dig plants out of a flat. Nutrients are built into the pot walls and carry the seedlings along during the early stages of growth.

The roll or carpet seedbeds, introduced in recent years, are made of batting or fiber impregnated with flower seeds. The material protects the seeds from birds and acts as a moisture-retentive mulch. However, you still have to prepare the soil that will be under the roll as thoroughly as you would for open ground seeding. Don't expect the seed in the matting to germinate and send its roots into hard packed soil.

Packaged potting soil, all mixed and ready to use, may be purchased in sacks at many nurseries. It saves you the time and bother of making up small quantities of potting soil when you don't have all the necessary raw materials on hand.

Some kinds of annual seed are now available in pelleted form. Each seed is coated with a material that disintegrates when the pellets are in place and moistened. The added bulk makes it easy to see and handle each seed individually and cuts down waste by allowing spaced sowing. Some seed coatings are colored to indicate flower color. Seed-starting procedure differs slightly from the regular method (you do not cover the pellets with soil); follow seed packet directions.

How to Prolong Bloom

The life cycle pattern of an annual is to grow, flower, set seed, and die, all in one season (in most cases). There is a point in each plant's development when tissues harden, growth stops, and the seed part of the cycle is triggered.

Hot weather hardens the tissues prematurely (this explains why many annuals planted in coastal gardens bloom longer than the same variety in a hot inland garden). Tissues harden if the supply of nutrients gives out before the plant is mature. Cold nights have the same effect; so do dessicating winds. Lack of water and damage to the plant by disease and certain pests are further contributing factors.

Anything you can do to prevent premature hardening of the plants will prolong bloom; and even after natural hardening has commenced, you can encourage more flowers to develop simply by removing the faded blossoms to prevent the development of any seeds.

Let's take a detailed look at some of the things you can do to forestall premature hardening of the tissues:

Select annuals known to grow well in your climate. For example, nasturtiums grow very well in cool climates; zinnias don't. The reverse is true in hot-summer areas.

Keep faded blooms picked off. Make the rounds at least once a week and snip them off.

Start feeding annuals almost as soon as they are in the ground, and feed regularly (every 2 weeks isn't too often). Water deeply, and repeat whenever the top inch or two of soil dries out. Use a mulch to conserve moisture, to reduce competition from weeds, and to keep the soil surface cool. A vigorous plant will help shade its own roots.

Spray to control pests and diseases. Sweet peas, for example, will bloom a month to 6 weeks longer if not

allowed to mildew. The same thing applies to calendulas and zinnias.

Stake taller growing plants such as asters, cleome, African marigolds, and snapdragons.

Pest Control

Pests and diseases take their toll of annual plantings regardless of where you garden. Snails and slugs chomp away at the leaves, diabroticas chew holes in leaves and flowers, aphids suck plant juices, red spider mites discolor foliage, and caterpillars try their best to outdo all the others. Whiteflies can be a real pest, and so can some of the soil-infesting insects that work out of sight on the roots or on the stems just below the surface.

Mildew plagues plantings in some areas, coating stems with a powdery matter.

However, it's far from an uphill battle. There are sprays and dusts that take care of just about any pest or disease that's likely to come along. With the multi-purpose dusts and sprays, you don't even have to know exactly which culprit is doing the damage. These sprays or dusts contain both an insecticide and a miticide.

You may need a fungicide to combat mildew. There are several good ones available; the best guide is to check labels; they'll tell you what the product will control. Once powdery mildew gets a foothold, it's not easy to control. So for best results, use a preventive dust or spray as soon as you notice it. In fact, many gardeners who keep records on annuals they plant and how they perform know from experience which plants get mildew and just about what time it usually hits. They schedule dusting and spraying accordingly.

WHEN YOU PULL OUT OLD ANNUALS, SHAKE DIRT OFF ROOTS

SPRAY BED WITH INSECTICIDE-FUNGICIDE

Snails and slugs do most damage to small seedlings or bedding plants and can be bad pests in some areas. However, there really isn't much sense putting up with them when the commercial snail and slug killers are so effective. The secret is to keep a supply of meal, pellets, dust, or spray on hand, and to use them regularly. The metaldehyde sprays and dusts cover the leaves and stems of the plants where the snails and slugs are most active. They have to come down to the ground to get the meal and pellets, which they may not do for days if the eating is good "upstairs."

Gophers and moles can ruin a bed of annuals in a few days. Gophers, common in many sections of the country, not only throw up mounds of soil that knock over and bury some plants and make a mess, but they find most annuals pretty tasty. On a windless day, you may see a plant begin to wave wildly back and forth, then suddenly disappear into the ground. There may be no evidence of earth mounds to warn you that gophers are at work.

Trapping is most effective and reassuring because you have the satisfaction of *knowing* you got the gopher. The traps have to be set well back into the main run, not in the short channels used to throw out dirt. Poisoned carrots and prunes work very well, but must be used with caution and are not recommended where pets or children may find the poisoned bait. There are also commercial baits and gases.

New subdivisions and country places are sure targets for gophers. The machinery and building activity in open fields or orchards drive the gophers into adjoining gardens where it's quieter. Then when the houses are built and the gardens are planted, gophers may move back into the new gardens in old runs so extensive that only a unified gopher campaign, with all neighbors cooperating, will be effective.

Moles are insectivorous and don't live on plants, much preferring the insects that live just under the soil surface. But their tunneling does disturb the plants as they burrow away with their powerful front feet and push up soil with their heads. The spear-type trap is most often used.

Annuals as Cut Flowers

One of the rewards of growing annuals is having an abundance of flowers to cut for the house. Even though you can buy many of these same flowers at florists or flower stalls, there is nothing so satisfying as picking armloads right out of your own garden. And, too, by growing some uncommon annuals—or less known varieties of familiar kinds—you have the fun of making arrangements that are refreshingly unique.

If one of your hobbies is growing your own cut flowers, you will find in this book many ideas for cutting and arranging them—under the descriptive material for the individual annuals. You'll find that most annuals can be used as cut flowers; and that many are excellent. However, a few are not at all suitable—you'll want to avoid those if you're thinking of planting a cut flower garden.

Of course, certain principles for the care of cut flowers apply to all kinds of plants, whether they're annuals, perennials, bulbs, shrubs, or trees. To avoid repetition throughout the book, we review these basic rules here. If you follow them, your arrangements should stay fresh considerably longer than they would otherwise.

When to pick flowers. The best time to pick flowers is in the early morning or in the cool of the evening when they are well filled with water. Never pick flowers from plants that are dry; water thoroughly a few days before you intend to pick the flowers.

How to cut flowers. A sharp knife makes the best tool for cutting flowers; pruning shears tend to crush the stem cells through which water is conducted. Make long slanting cuts to increase the amount of surface through which water is admitted. With larger, heavier stems, it is helpful to slit them up about an inch from the base. Cut stems as long as possible; shorten them as needed when you put the arrangements together.

For a more interesting arrangement, pick flowers in various stages of development—in full bloom, partly opened, and in bud. Some flowers, of course, should be picked at a particular stage in order to keep satisfactorily; this information is included, when it applies, under specific flowers.

Leaves can often become an important part of an arrangement; pick some along with the flowers to which they belong.

After cutting. Immediately after cutting, place the flowers in a deep container filled with cold water. Some gardeners carry a pail or can of water with them into the garden and place each stem in the water as they cut. Remove leaves at the bottom of the stems that will be submerged in the water, since they discolor the water, encourage bacteria formation, and cause unpleasant odor. Let the flowers stand in deep water for several hours, or even better, overnight.

Column of soft pink double hollyhock is foil for airy white baby's breath, spikes of white physostegia.

In color, form, and keeping qualities, Bells of Ireland (here with dahlias) are almost in a class by themselves.

Special treatment after cutting. Certain flowers, such as poppies and members of the euphorbia family, require special treatment in order to keep well. Severed stems of these flowers exude a slimy or milky juice; to prevent this ooze from clogging the narrow water-conducting tubes in the plants' stems, seal the cuts by searing them in a flame, or dipping them in boiling water for a second or two. If you place them in water right after treatment, flowers will keep fresh —often for several days—while those that are not treated will wilt rapidly.

Flowers need air. Don't stuff them tightly into containers. Arrange them loosely enough so that oxygen can reach the water.

Daily care. Cut flowers keep best in a cool place— at a temperature of about 50° (not much below); room temperatures, of course, are usually considerably higher so that they will be comfortable for human occupants. However, even in a fairly warm room, many cut flowers will remain in good condition for several days if you do as follows:

1. Re-cut the stems once a day. This will remove the bacteria that develop on the cut surface of the stem and clog the water-carrying vessels. A helpful trick, especially for flowers with small conducting cells in their stems, is to re-cut the stems under water. (Again, remember to remove any leaves that might be submerged.)

2. Remove faded flowers promptly to keep the arrangement looking fresh and tidy, and to make room for buds that may be ready to unfold.

3. Change the water in the container daily to slow down the formation of bacteria and prevent odor. If you don't find it convenient to change the water completely, add sufficient fresh water to replace that which has evaporated. An easy way to remove stale water without dislodging the arrangement is to siphon it out with a bulb syringe.

4. Keep the arrangement out of drying drafts, direct sunlight, and currents of hot air. Place it in a cool place during the night.

Artificial preservatives. Over the past several years, there have been introduced various commercial products recommended by their manufacturers as useful in prolonging the life of cut flowers. Flower arrangers have used them with varying degrees of success; however, most experienced arrangers seem to feel that in the long run, following the practices suggested above are generally more helpful than the addition of chemicals or other materials to the water.

Many cut flowers can also be preserved in their natural color and form for years by drying them in sand or some other desiccating medium. This fascinating procedure is outlined in complete detail in a companion *Sunset* book, *The Art of Flower Preservation* by Geneal Condon.

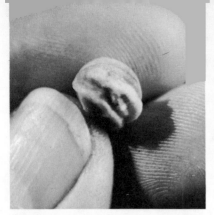

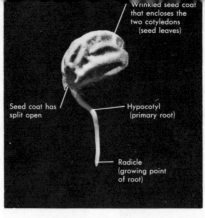

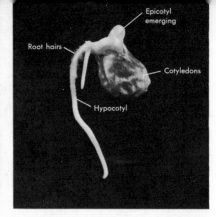

1 *Wrinkled nasturtium seed, approximately twice actual size.*

2 *First activity — seed coat splits and the hypocotyl appears.*

3 *Primary root grows downward; and the epicotyl emerges.*

4 *Cotyledons developing below soil is called hypogeous germination.*

5 *Stem now reaches the surface and begins to push through.*

6 *Above ground, first sign of germination is tiny stem's appearance.*

RICHARD DAWSON

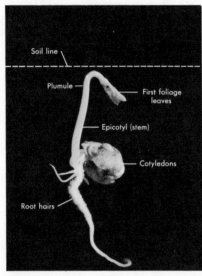

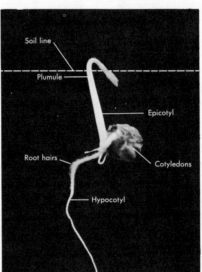

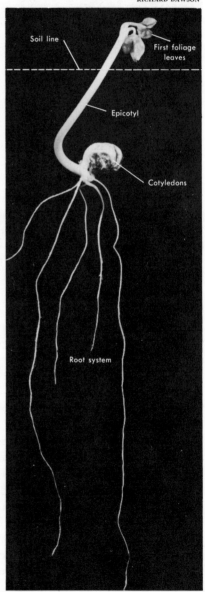

A SEED GERMINATES

Have you ever watched a seed germinate — go through that wonderful transformation from an apparently insignificant bit of matter into a living plant?

To get the photographic sequence shown here, a half dozen nasturtium seeds (they're big and easy to see) were sandwiched in folded pieces of moist paper towels on a dish. The dish was placed in a warm, dark closet until the first seed showed some sign of life.

Most annual flower seeds you're likely to grow in your garden take between one and three weeks to germinate. If the seed is viable it will germinate, but *when* it germinates depends on a rather fine balance of both external and internal factors. Moisture, temperature, and oxygen must be available in just the right amounts; then many changes take place simultaneously within the seed. The seed takes in water, the seed coat softens, and the seed swells. Enzyme activity increases, dissolving stored food and making it available to the growing embryo. The photographs here show you what happens next.

FLOWER STRUCTURE

One of the surest ways to raise the ire of a botanist is to show him a calendula, zinnia, or any other member of the Compositae family and call it a flower. To the layman it is a flower, but technically it is a whole head of many flowers, and often of two different kinds.

What you pull off as a "petal" is really a single flower known as a ray. This ray flower narrows to a tiny tube at the base. If there are two or three points (lobes) at the tip, then it's made up of two or three fused petals (corolla); sometimes there may be four or five. Ray flowers are around the outside of the flower head. The cushion-like center of the head is made up of many tiny flowers known as disc flowers. They're tubular with four or five points, each point representing a petal. Usually the disc flowers bear four or five pollen-bearing stamens in the center.

As a general rule (there are exceptions), ray flowers are either female or sterile. If they are female, they rely on the pollen from the disc flowers to set seed. The seeds are formed below the tiny ray flower tubes. If the ray flowers are sterile, then seed is produced by the disc flowers beneath the disc flower tube. Disc flowers may be only male, but more often both sexes are borne in the disc flower and these will usually set seed.

Some of the popular annuals and perennials that belong to the Compositae include asters, calendulas, chrysanthemums, coreopsis, cosmos, dahlias, daisies, gaillardia, marguerites, marigolds, sunflowers, Transvaal daisies, yarrows, and zinnias.

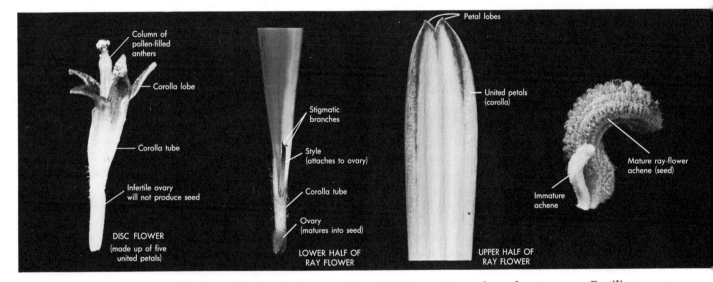

Before seed is formed in ray, pollen from disc flower must get to stigma of ray. Pollen grain forms tube that grows through style carrying male nucleus to ovary. Fertilization occurs when male nucleus contacts female nucleus.

A cross-section through the head shows location of the ray flowers and the disc flowers.

RICHARD DAWSON

A "flower" of the Compositae family is actually a head of two different kinds of flowers.

DARROW M. WATT

HOW TO USE COLOR

WHEN YOU PLANT a garden, you do more than set out annuals, perennials, trees, shrubs, or bulbs. You also work with colors—much as the artist or the interior designer works with them.

Annuals are a mainstay of the garden color enthusiast. Combining them in the garden isn't much different from working out a color scheme for a room. And with all the new flower colors developed in recent years, you can get almost the same variety of colors and subtle shades as you can from a paint color wheel or a group of fabric swatches.

Get to Know the Color Wheel

Working out basic color ideas for your garden can really be quite a simple matter, once you become familiar with the color wheel on the facing page. Here are the basic color relationships:

Complementary. Colors that face each other across the color wheel—like red and green—are called com-

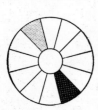

plementary. When you mix paints in two of these opposing or complementary colors, they neutralize, or complement, each other and make a shade of gray. But when the two complementary colors are placed side by side, as in a fabric, they contrast strongly with each other.

Harmonious. Now look at the colors that lie between the three primary colors. Note that according

to their position on the wheel, they are graduated mixtures of the primary colors on either side. These adjoining colors are obviously related, and in color language we call them harmonious. The closer together they are, the less they differ in color.

Warm or cool. You will note that the color wheel has warm and cool sections. For most people the warm section centers on orange and the cool section centers on blue.

Light to dark in value. This color wheel demonstrates that an individual color has a range of differ-

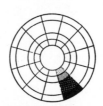

ent values from light to dark. The "true" color is in the center of each color wedge. It becomes gradually lighter in value toward the center as it is mixed with more and more white, darker toward the outside of the circle as it is mixed with more and more black.

Gray. Probably one of the most important of all colors found in plants is gray. Just as gray is produced by mixing opposing (complementary) colors, so it is the means of bridging the gap between these colors.

Applying the Basic Principles

With the above principles in mind, let's look at some of the ways you can apply them in your garden.

Contrasts. Every garden needs a few contrasts—for gaiety, exhilaration, excitement. You can play plants in complementary or contrasting colors against each other, or let plants supply one color and the background the other. Brilliant red salvia against a bright green hedge is a good example of the latter.

Go easy—too much use of contrast can make a garden appear restless and spotty. Contrasts are most effective when you use them as accents or foils to quieter, modulated harmonies. Remember, too, that all contrasts need not necessarily be vivid; use subdued and neutral shades for soft contrast.

Harmonies. You can develop some wonderful harmonies with closely related colors from the warm or cool side of the color wheel. For example, asters, petunias, and sweet peas can give you a good range of blues, as well as warm pinks, reds, and violet. Select varieties by color.

Subordination. In garden color schemes, as in interiors and costuming, there should be a single dominant color to which all other colors are subordinate. At most times of the year, green—which appears, of course, in an almost infinite range—is the dominant garden color. In spring, yellow becomes much more in evidence; in autumn, the warm colors come on strong.

In the long run, how you use color will depend on your personal preferences and your reaction to various colors, but a color wheel is useful to establish some basic facts about color and color relationships.

The three primary colors, of course, are red, yellow, and blue. Equally spaced around the color wheel, they form a triangle. If you were to make a color wheel yourself, you could do it by combining the primary colors as follows:

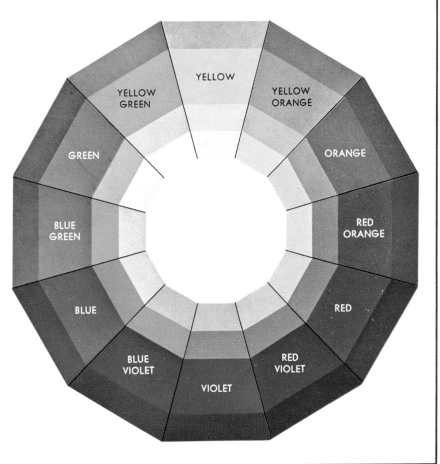

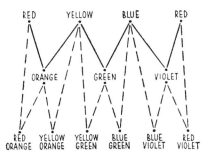

In this complementary combination, blue forget-me-not is subordinate to yellow Achillea taggetea.

These colors are in harmony. Orange snapdragons, yellow marigolds are related warm colors of high intensity.

ERNEST BRAUN

LANDSCAPING WITH ANNUALS

IN THIS CHAPTER we recognize annuals as landscape material of a very special nature: as plants to delight the gardener who enjoys color and finds no end of satisfaction in working out different combinations of colors; and as practical, easy problem-solvers in situations found in many home gardens. At the end of the chapter, you will find information on another important facet of growing annuals: their use as container plants.

Color Combinations

Here are some effective combinations of annuals used by themselves and with other kinds of plants:

- Blue petunias with blue ageratum and lobelia.
- One color in a border through an entire season — for example, yellows. Calendulas and yellow violas for the cool months of late winter and spring, marigolds or zinnias for summer and fall.
- A round bed filled with maroon, plumy celosias surrounded by orange marigolds, with an edging of blue ageratum.
- With a dwarf pomegranate hedge, dwarf yellow marigolds with an edging of the miniature single orange marigolds (*Tagetes tenuifolia pumila*).
- Dwarf citrus with *Sedum praealtum* and orange or yellow calendulas or dwarf marigolds.
- Old-fashioned lavender heliotrope with purple petunias.
- Purple sweet alyssum edging around a wide band of dwarf yellow marigolds, with the center filled with white petunias.

Interplanted near a front entry, lemon yellow marigolds and blue lobelia team up for a dazzling color show. In the background is foundation planting of Daphne odora *and* Pieris japonica. *Rail is of wrought-iron.*

Front gardens of hillside homes can be enhanced greatly by mass plantings of annuals, perennials, bulbs, shrubs, and trees. For maximum enjoyment, choose plants that bloom at different times of the year.

- Pink snapdragons with a border of pink and white sweet alyssum.
- Dwarf yellow marigolds as a border for magenta globe amaranth.
- Rose beds edged with annual pinks and sweet alyssum.
- Crimson bougainvillea on a trellis underplanted with blue ageratum and deep purple petunias.
- Red salvia border against a background of tall soft yellow marigolds or white zinnias.
- A bed of white petunias with islands of pink or purple petunias, each island consisting of about three plants.
- Pink sweet alyssum woven between blue lobelia, blue viola, purple nierembergia, or blue ageratum.
- Yellow and apricot gladiolus with yellow, apricot, and bronze snapdragons. For contrast, add a group of brilliant blue Chinese forget-me-nots.
- Mixed nicotiana in pinks, red, and white, behind impatiens or torenia.
- In the background, plant deep rose-colored cosmos; next, interplant pink or white cleome. Add an

Free-flowering sweet William, in sparkling shades of pink and red, is a good choice for a mixed flower border.

edging of pink or white petunias.

• Lavender and purple stock as a background for pale blue lace flower. In front, set out double-flowered dwarf balsam in shades of pink and rose-red and white.

• Yellow hollyhocks, blue larkspur, blue cornflower, with pale salmon-pink godetia or salmon-rose dwarf zinnia.

Small-Garden Borders

In many small gardens where planting space is limited, flowers must often be confined to borders or strips (usually 3 to 4 feet wide). Such a border should not only be gay and colorful for several months, but should also provide cut flowers for the house. The following combinations will meet these needs:

Plant mixed penstemons 15 to 18 inches apart. Then, every 3 or 4 feet, interplant annual white baby's breath. If the border is 4 feet wide or more, you will have room to plant a row of dwarf Chinese delphinium (the deep blue variety gives the most striking effect) in front, with some white sweet alys-

sum directly along the edge. The baby's breath will hold its airy flowers slightly higher than the penstemons, just as it would in a bouquet.

Many flower bowls may be filled from a planting that includes mixed cosmos, green- and white-leafed snow-on-the-mountain, and pink or rose annual phlox.

Fence Planting

A tall redwood or cedar fence or a white wall will provide a good setting for the spectacular reddish-orange daisy flowers of tithonia (variously called Mexican sunflower, tree zinnia, and golden flower of the Incas), red and orange zinnias, and scarlet and gold salpiglossis. Don't leave too little space for this sun-loving planting—tithonias will grow to 8 feet, and spread out to 6 feet.

Here is a fence planting in blue, yellow, and orange: Sow seed of 'Heavenly Blue' morning glory

To right of walk are white and purple alyssum, zinnias, scarlet sage; giant ruffled petunias are on left.

directly against the fence; in front, plant orange zinnias, with an edging of dwarf yellow marigolds.

Ground Covers

Low-growing annuals make ideal ground covers between newly planted shrubs and trees that have not yet become well established or attained full size. In large gardens, the best solution is to scatter seed of wildflowers or of easy annuals.

For a stunning effect, sow a ground cover of pink sweet alyssum around Floribunda roses 'White Bouquet', 'Ivory Fashion', 'Pinkie', 'The Fairy' (shell pink), or 'Lavender Girl'.

Annuals as Problem-Solvers

Here are some common garden problems and a few of the annuals that will help you solve them. Keep one thing in mind: These recommendations are not intended to put a halter on your imagination; there are dozens of other excellent annuals that will do the job.

Bare spots in bulb beds. If you grow bulbs, you have the problem of what to do for color when the flowers are gone and the foliage begins to fade. Annuals planted now will fill in as the bulb foliage withers. They will also leave the ground free for working with the bulbs in fall and spring. Choose

Featured in this raised bed planting are three of the annuals featured in the "all-time favorites" chapter (see page 32). From front to rear: lobelia, marigolds, petunias. Grapestake fence provides neutral background.

Scarlet, rose, yellow-orange nemesias are planted in front of columbine; grape hyacinth, gerbera in foreground.

Tall-growing cosmos, in shades of red, rose, pink, and white, relieve the monotony of a long wooden fence.

Sunken lawn is surrounded by extensive mixed planting of annuals, perennials, bulbs, and woody plants.

Solid planting of stock, with white alyssum edging, grows in front of low, rustic fence leading to entry gate.

annuals adapted to the bulb's requirements for sun and for dry conditions as it matures. *Recommended:* marigold, zinnia, poppy.

Sparse look of new shrub plantings. When you start a foundation planting, shrub border, or a hedge, the planting may look pretty bare for the first year or so. Use annuals for temporary fillers. Choose bushy types that won't spread and take over the planting. *Recommended:* snapdragons, stock.

Lack of color in shrub border. Annuals can do a lot to keep a shrub border interesting after its flowers have faded. Choose vigorous plants that carry bloom high enough to be seen. *Recommended:* larkspur, nicotiana, salpiglossis, cosmos, cleome, hollyhock, foxglove.

Walks, drives, beds that need borders. Among the best edging and border plants are annuals. Some are neat and formal looking, others are informal. *Recommended:* sweet alyssum, nemesia, dwarf marigold (formal); petunia, annual phlox (informal).

A difficult dry location. Large lots and country places, especially, will frequently have corners or sections that are difficult to water. What you need here is one of the annuals that manages to do very nicely with minimum watering or occasional normal rainfall. *Recommended:* verbena, nasturtium, portulaca.

Fast-Growing Vines

Vines that grow from seed to maturity in a hurry can fill an important need in many gardens. They give an immediate, spectacular effect, covering very large areas inside of six or eight weeks. They serve as fast, inexpensive fillers while you plan your permanent planting. Or they may give you shade from the hot afternoon sun or a covering for a wall.

Some of the most popular and useful annual vines are: sweet pea, morning glory (also effective for covering an unsightly, steep bank), scarlet runner bean, nasturtium, and cardinal climber.

Annuals in Containers

Many patios, terraces, decks, and porches would lose much of their charm if it weren't for the warmth and cheer of colorful annuals growing in pots, tubs, boxes, hanging baskets, and other containers.

ERNEST BRAUN

Spikes of luminous yellow snapdragons contrast with the round, flat heads of pink sweet William. White sweet alyssum sounds a crisp, clear, contrasting note.

Yet one shouldn't be overly nonchalant about approaching this pleasant avocation—annuals growing in containers definitely require more care than those growing in the open ground. Roots confined in a small space have less soil area from which to draw nutrients, and dry out faster: to compensate, it is necessary to weed and water the plants more generously and regularly.

Annuals grown in containers also need better grooming, since there is obviously little point in displaying unattractive plants. Actually, upkeep isn't as tedious as it may sound. If you develop the habit of removing faded flowers or leaves with one hand, while holding the hose or watering can with the other, you systematically combine grooming and watering into a single simple operation.

Soil mixture. A loose, porous, spongy soil mixture is generally most satisfactory for the majority of annuals—just as it is for other kinds of plants. The mixture should drain easily, yet hold enough moisture so as not to dry out too rapidly on warm days.

In general, a satisfactory mix should contain one-half sandy loam and one-half leaf mold, peat moss, ground bark, or similar humous material, with complete fertilizer added according to label directions. If you use a heavy soil, increase the amount of humus. Gardeners who use rotted manure in the soil mixture may reduce the amount of complete fertilizer, or omit it.

Planting techniques. Most annuals you see displayed in containers have been transplanted into them from flats, bands, or peat pots. Among the exceptions are such annuals as sweet alyssum, linaria, nasturtium, and Virginian stock which are generally sown where they are to grow — both in the open ground and in containers. These annuals are often

In the foreground at the top of an informal rock wall is planting of 'Comanche' petunias (All-America). Among the petunias is a plant of geum, with orange flowers. Lavender-blue ageratum flowers grow in front.

'Ballerina' petunias (All-America) make an effective curving border. On other side of walk are zinnias.

Violas combine with alyssum in front of young shrubs—a good example of how annuals can be used as fillers.

sown as ground covers at the base of container-grown trees, shrubs, or bulbs.

To get a generous mass effect, plant more closely in containers than in the ground. For instance, instead of setting petunias 10 to 12 inches apart, as in a border in the garden, you might set them 4 inches apart—3 plants, let us say, in a 7-inch pot. Or, put as many as 5 lobelia plants in a 6-inch pot—4 plants near the edge of the pot, and one in the center.

Certain annuals, of course, require ample space even in containers, and shouldn't be planted too closely. Cinerarias, for example, should be planted one to a pot; their rounded, mounding form calls for it, their roots resent crowding, and their water needs are critical. Butterfly flower is another annual that needs plenty of room in order to do its best.

In general, it's a good idea to make a light monthly application of complete fertilizer, preferably in readily available liquid form, starting a month or so after potting and continuing until flowers start to bloom. Discontinue after plants are in full flower.

Some Favorite Annuals For Containers

Although most annuals can be grown in containers, some seem better adapted to this purpose than others. Following are 20 that many gardeners have found satisfactory.

Ageratum. Combine dwarf varieties with petunias or annual phlox, or interplant with white or pink sweet alyssum.

Alyssum. All varieties of sweet alyssum make quick effective ground covers or edgings for taller plants in containers. Sow in place, or set out plants from flats.

Browallia. One of the best for long lasting summer and fall color in partial shade. Attractive in groupings with tuberous begonias, fuchsias, and hydrangeas.

Butterfly flower. Pastel flowered plants are charming alone or with fairy primroses, cinerarias, or blue or white violas.

Cineraria. When well grown, a spectacular container plant for shady outdoor areas in frost-free climates. Group with pots of browallia, coleus, lobelia, or nicotiana.

Coleus. Its colorful foliage brightens patios and

A low mat of floriferous, brilliant red verbenas is highlight of this planting. Near verbena are Festuca glauca, juniper, agave, and ajuga. In background next to house are Phormium tenax and Aralia sieboldii. Large rock adds interesting design element.

terraces in summer. Coleus is also a very popular house plant.

Dianthus. For a fresh, jaunty effect, surround a pot or boxful of dianthus with an edging of 'Carpet of Snow' sweet alyssum.

Fairy primrose. In mild climates, one of the most effective plants for spring color in containers. Try with daffodils, hyacinths, tulips, other spring flowering bulbs.

Impatiens. Both *I. holstii* and *I. sultanii* are fine container plants for partial shade during the summer and early fall months.

Lobelia. Invaluable for containers, particularly as an accompaniment to other plants.

Marigold. Dwarf varieties are especially serviceable long-blooming container plants.

Mignonette. If you want fragrance close by, grow mignonette in a pot or box near your door. Sow seed directly in the container.

Mimulus. 'Queen's Prize' is a colorful, unusual plant for containers in shaded areas.

Nasturtium. Among the easiest annuals to grow in pots. Sow the seeds directly in the container; thin to the desired number of plants.

Nicotiana. White nicotiana is especially appealing for its fragrance and cool appearance on summer evenings.

Petunia. Invaluable for all kinds of containers. Balcony (trailing) varieties best for hanging baskets and pots. Give light afternoon shade in hot summer climates.

Phlox. Set annual phlox rather thickly in boxes, tubs, or large pots. Dwarf varieties are most satisfactory since they are less inclined to sprawl.

Torenia. Dainty plant for close-up containers in partial shade. Combine with light and darker blue lobelia.

Viola. As invaluable for spring and early summer color in containers as it is in the ground. Blue or white violas are compatible with almost anything.

Virginian stock. For a multi-colored carpet under trees, shrubs, or with taller annuals in containers.

Annuals can provide breathtaking sights in large gardens, if used lavishly and yet with careful planting. Pansies grow next to lawn. Stocks (just coming into bloom) are behind them. Presiding over all of this is a row of stately snapdragons. Warm colors predominate.

Alyssum 'Rosie O'Day' (All-America) is planted along walkway. In background are lavender-blue violas.

Unusual but effective scheme: Gravel walk, bordered by geraniums, is flanked by six-sided beds of snapdragons.

Corner planting of red and gold 'Old Mexico' zinnias (All-America), backed by large-flowered varieties.

GALLERY OF FLOWERS

THE ILLUSTRATIONS on these two pages are a sampling of annuals described in the encyclopedia section (see pages 60 to 78). They were selected with two primary thoughts in mind: to show the variety of flower and plant forms you can choose from, and to give an idea of the almost limitless color range.

Cosmos (See page 67)   *Salpiglossis (See page 76)*   *Dahlia—Unwin's (See page 68)*

Phlox—Globe Mixed (All-America) (See page 74)   *Larkspur—Giant Imperial Mixed (See page 71)*

Aster—Giant Crego   (See page 62)

Morning Glory 'Heavenly Blue'   (See page 73)

Dianthus 'Bravo' (All-America) (See page 68)

Ageratum (See page 60)

Celosia (Cockscomb)   (See page 65)

Iceland Poppy   (See page 75)

A DOZEN FAVORITES

THE POPULAR ANNUALS described in this chapter may or may not be your own favorites. However, these selections — from Alyssum through Zinnia — do represent a cross-section of annuals with certain things in their favor.

All of them, for example, rate high on the list of best sellers — and have for many years. All are colorful, free-flowering, and relatively easy to grow.

If you never have grown annuals, try some of these "all-timers" as a starter. Once they are familiar to you, the others listed in the encyclopedia section (see page 60) will offer many exciting alternatives.

Marigold 'Crackerjack'
(See page 37)

Snapdragon—F₁ Hybrid Rockets
(See page 49)

Pansy
(See page 42)

Sweet Pea (See page 53)

Zinnia—Dahlia Flowered (See page 56)

Petunia 'White Magic'(See page 44)

All-Time Favorites:

ALYSSUM

Annual sweet alyssum is one plant that gives you full return on your money and gardening time. It grows quickly and surely (six weeks from seed to bloom) in most garden soils, and will continue to bloom for many months. It requires only minimum watering. It's not a plant you have to use with restraint; it looks best in broad bands or drifts. The tiny flowers have a delightful, honey-like fragrance.

A trio of low growers in a raised bed: alyssum, ageratum, and dwarf annual phlox; also ideal for along a path.

As a low edging plant, it's hard to beat. It fills in around the base of shrubs, perennials, and other annuals. It makes a fast filler between rocks on a bank or in a rock garden while more permanent plants are getting established. Sweet alyssum is very attractive as a cover in a bed of spring blooming bulbs, and it will help to hide the bulb's drying foliage in late spring. It's a life-saver for the gardener who moves into a new and unlandscaped place and yearns for some plants that grow *right now*.

Culture

Sweet alyssum is a hardy, sun-loving annual that does well in ordinary garden soil. Seed germinates in about a week in spring or fall if the weather is warm; a little slower if the soil is cool and wet. Summer seeding is not generally too satisfactory.

Broadcast the seed where it is to grow (the usual method), or start it in flats and transplant it later. In either case, you'll get better coverage if you first mix the tiny seed with some sand.

Work up the bed before you sow the seed. Although we've seen volunteer plants growing right out of a compacted gravel path, sweet alyssum will do better

Alyssum 'Carpet of Snow' was sown when tree roses were set out in spring; new sowings may be made annually.

if it gets off to a good start. If you've just finished planting bulbs and want to sow a cover of sweet alyssum, smooth off the bed with a rake, sow the seed, rake it in lightly (or barely cover it with peat moss, sand, or sifted compost), then water gently with a fine spray.

In flats you can sow the seed in ¼-inch drills, or broadcast it over the surface and sift ¼-inch of sand or peat moss over the seed. Firm the seed in with a board or brick. Then water the flat.

You can also buy plants in flats. Sweet alyssum is set back two or three weeks by transplanting, unless a ball of soil is kept intact around the roots.

Sweet alyssum will flower for many months, straight through the winter in mild sections. It is difficult to tell just how long a single plant blooms because new plants are always coming up. Pull old ones when seed clusters turn brown.

White and purple alyssum, planted on a bank, poke up through garden steps to lend an informal effect.

Lobelia and white alyssum make a cushiony, blue and white carpet for 'Heavenly Blue' morning glory.

Most people don't think of sweet alyssum as a cut flower, but you sometimes see the fragrant white blooms in miniature bouquets—with other dainty flowers such as English daisies, baby roses, and forget-me-nots.

Kinds You Can Get

The old-fashioned sweet alyssum is white and grows 8 to 10 inches high. Seed of this is still available, but some of the newer named forms, lower growing

(about 4 inches) and more compact, have become more popular in recent years. You can also get forms with violet or purple flowers; some seed packets contain a mixture of violet and white, a very attractive combination in the garden.

Some good low-growing varieties: 'Carpet of Snow', a pure white; 'Royal Carpet' (All-America), rich purple, deepening in cool weather; 'Rosie O'Day' (All-America), soft rose pink in cool weather, lavender-pink in summer.

All-white border starts at edge of lawn with white sweet alyssum, then white violas backed by white marguerites.

Border around iris was made by interplanting white and purple sweet alyssum—'Carpet of Snow,' 'Royal Carpet.'

All-Time Favorites:

CALENDULAS

This immensely popular cool-season annual is sometimes referred to as "pot marigold"—but a marigold it is not (see page 37 for information on the true marigolds). The calendula is a plant unto itself, and ranks as one of the most universal of garden flowers.

In mild-climate areas, and particularly in California, calendula is perhaps the outstanding winter blooming standby. Gardens that might otherwise be fresh out of flower color following the departure of autumn suddenly take on new life as the pale yellow to warm orange flowers begin their show. Mass plantings are most effective.

In mild climates, if you plant them early enough (prior to Labor Day) these sturdily built annuals will bloom before Christmas and will continue to bloom well into spring.

Plants are bushy and grow to 2 feet in warm weather; during the winter a low, leafy rosette is formed, topped by 12-inch flower stems. The leaves are long, narrow, and slightly sticky. The double, semi-double, or single flowers are usually borne one to a stem.

Culture

Seed of calendulas may be sown in flats or directly where plants are to grow. For early color, plant in full sun; in desert areas, give them light shade.

The seeds will germinate in about a week. When seedlings are well on their way, thin them so the plants will be 12 inches apart.

In mild-climate regions, sow the seeds in July or August for winter bloom, and in September or October for spring bloom. Where winters are cold, either start them in greenhouses in winter and plant out very carefully in spring, or sow seed in early summer for color in late summer and fall.

Richness of soil is not a factor, but it is important that the soil be well drained. Occasional cultivation is also beneficial. Water regularly, but don't overdo it.

Pinch back the main stem when the first flower head starts to form; this encourages branching and thus results in more flowers.

Occasional infestations of cabbage worms or aphids can be controlled easily by using a multi-purpose insecticide. Snails and slugs relish the fresh fall foliage; control with meal or pellet bait.

Yellow and orange calendulas are good choice for plantings next to the house. Snapdragons provide tall accents.

Good Cut Flowers

Calendulas are good cut flowers if picked in bud or near-bud. When picked in full bloom, flowers shatter and wilt within a short time. They are effective with substantial green foliage; also with blue bachelor buttons. Old-fashioned orange or yellow calendulas look bright and cheerful in a brown bean pot or a simple copper or pottery bowl.

Varieties

The Pacific Beauty class contains clear colors; 'Flame' and 'Persimmon' are excellent. Mixture includes yellow, cream, and apricot shades.

Calendula's flowers are quite similar to those of some marigolds—hence the alternate name, "pot marigold."

All-Time Favorites:

LOBELIA

Lobelia 'Cambridge Blue' (foreground) combines with salmon-pink godetia and sky blue Chinese delphinium.

This versatile free-flowering low grower (4 to 8 inches) is one of the most popular summer annuals in areas where summers are cool. It comes in both compact and trailing forms, with foliage that is light, medium, or dark green, often tying in with light, medium, or dark blue flowers.

Lobelia offers some excellent possibilities for planting in partly shaded areas. Use it as an edging or as a ground cover; or in pots, window boxes, or hanging baskets. Trailing forms are most popular for containers because they are so graceful spilling down over the sides of a pot or box. Compact forms will do almost the same thing, but the slender stems aren't as long.

If you grow lobelia in pots, you can use them to brighten your patio; or, you can move them out in the yard to give a lift to shady corner plantings. Consider placing pots of flowering lobelia at the base of a container-grown hydrangea, or grouping them with tuberous or fibrous begonias, fuchsias, or cinerarias.

Try spotting in some light blue lobelia throughout a planting of succulents in early spring; simply thin out the succulents enough to make room for the lobelia. The light blue of lobelia and the blue-green foliage of hen-and-chickens *(Sempervivum tectorum)* is particularly effective. Remove the lobelia when it finishes flowering or becomes leggy. By this time the succulents will have spread out considerably.

Culture

If you live in an area where spring comes early, you may sow seed directly outdoors. However, lobelia is a little slow to reach maturity from seed, and you may prefer to do what most gardeners do: buy young plants from a nursery when spring's warm weather comes, or start the seeds indoors in winter in a greenhouse or coldframe (it takes nearly 2 months for the seeds to grow to planting-out size). Some gardeners in climates with no-frost winters start seed in May for fall and winter color.

Set out plants 9 inches apart, in a sunny location or in part shade, and in a rich, moist soil. Lobelia will take full sun if it gets enough water, but plants appear more lush and flower colors more intense if you put them in part shade. If you live in a cool-summer region, a sunny location is preferable.

After the first main blooming period, shear back the plants lightly. This will keep them blooming through summer and well into fall.

Varieties

'Crystal Palace' (dark blue flowers, bronze foliage), 'Cambridge Blue' (light blue flowers, green foliage), 'Mrs. Clibran' (dark blue flowers, white eye; dark foliage), 'Rosamond' (violet-rose flowers, white eye; medium-green foliage), 'White Lady' (pure white flowers, green foliage), 'Sapphire' (azure blue flowers, green foliage). The latter is a trailing type, wonderful for hanging baskets; try combining it with hanging fuchsias, ivy geranium, or trailing white campanula.

Lobelia is effective in containers. Trailing forms are most popular; compact forms are also good pot subjects.

All-Time Favorites:

MARIGOLDS

Marigolds—the flowers you see on the cover of this book—are the flower gardener's mainstay. Beginners like them for several reasons: plants grow quickly and easily from seed; they come in every size from 6 inches to 3 feet high; they are seldom bothered by pests or diseases; they bloom without let-up through the summer into fall, furnishing quantities of gaily colored cut flowers for the house.

Experienced gardeners usually maintain a lively interest in marigolds because there are so many interesting kinds to choose from. Tantalizing new varieties are being introduced almost constantly.

Wherever you put marigolds, their gay colors will catch the eye. They come in many shades of yellow, orange, dark reds and maroon—or in combinations of these colors. Use them with a bold hand, massing them in drifts or bays, the small ones up front and tall forms in the background. Try them with an edging of blue lobelia or ageratum. Grow them in containers, raised beds, or among shrubs that are still too small to make a show.

S. C. WILSON

Double-flowered golden yellow marigolds make a gay border against fence; lawn in front provides contrast.

If there are blank spots in your garden and you are looking for a quick and effective fill-in, consider marigolds. For an immediate effect, set out plants from flats. If you can anticipate your needs, plant seed in the open ground. When seeding, keep in mind that even before they bloom they will make a bare piece

S. C. WILSON

Mass planting of 'Man in the Moon' marigolds is effective here as a colorful backing for a terrace.

of ground look like part of the garden. As soon as the plants are up—about 2 weeks after sowing seed—their young leaves form a green carpet.

Culture

No annuals grow more easily from seed than marigolds. The seeds are easy to handle and they germinate readily (in 7 days, or less in warm weather). You can start them in flats if you wish, but many gardeners plant them in the ground directly where they are to grow. Be sure to give them a sunny location.

If you prefer to buy young plants at a nursery, you will probably find that there are several varieties to choose from. Most of them look pretty much alike at this stage, but be sure to find out whether the ones you select are tall, medium, or short varieties. Smaller kinds should be planted about 6 inches apart; larger types should be planted farther apart—up to 18 inches if you are growing the big fellows.

French (dwarf) marigolds actually flower best in a rather poor soil. It is important not to overwater them. The African marigold, on the other hand, needs a rich, well-prepared soil and plenty of water. Be sure water penetrates the matted root area.

No matter which type you are growing, it is best not to water the foliage as a regular practice. An occasional light spray early in the day won't hurt them—the water will soon evaporate. However, continuous overhead watering can cause full-grown

Dwarf single marigolds make a golden edging. Also, interplant them with purple alyssum or blue lobelia.

Yellow, maroon-spotted 'Naughty Marietta' dwarf marigolds brighten a terrace in place of eight dry-laid bricks.

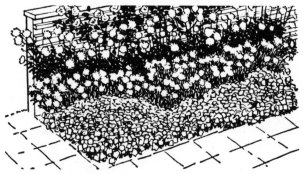

Tall marigolds planted in front of yellow climbing rose. In front: lavender-blue scabiosa, purple nierembergia.

Dwarf marigolds, planted in a drift near driveway and path to house, make a delightful summer border.

plants to bend under the water's weight, and some of the stems may snap (marigold stems tend to be brittle).

Pinch back African marigolds when they are about 8 inches high so they won't get leggy; pinching encourages branching and thus results in heavier flower production.

Good Cut Flowers

Marigolds are popular cut flowers, lasting for many days; some people object to their odor indoors. A good way to arrange them is with green foliage, such as that of euonymus, privet, or viburnum. Be sure to remove marigolds' bottom leaves to avoid contaminating the water.

Kinds and Varieties

French (dwarf): The Petites rate as the outstanding double flowered types. They grow to 8 inches high, and are outstanding for neat, trim edgings. Colors include yellow, orange, gold, and mixed. 'Petite Harmony' is brown and gold. Dwarf singles, taller than the Petites, are stronger plants, good for bedding 'Flash' (All-America) is russet with gold markings; 'Dainty Marietta' is yellow and brown.

African (dwarf): Plants are middle-sized, 12-18 inches. Flowers are 2-2½ inches across. 'Cupid', available in yellow, orange, or a mixture of these colors, is a good variety.

Dwarf French marigolds grow to only 8 inches high; good as foreground for plantings along a driveway.

All-marigold "step" planting: 'Lemon Drop' (9 inches), 'Naughty Marietta' (15 in.), 'Man in the Moon' (3 ft.).

African (tall): Most African marigolds are tall (to 3 feet) and late-blooming. 'Crackerjack' is a mid-season bloomer; it has double flowers 3-4 inches across, and is available in mixed colors. The new F_1 hybrids are superior to older varieties of African marigold. 'Climax', in yellow, orange, gold, and primrose, blooms by midsummer; flowers are 4-5 inches across, and plants are uniform and covered with blooms from top to bottom. 'Sahara' has slightly larger blossoms and comes into bloom 2 weeks later.

Dwarf single: Entirely distinct from French types. Fern-like foliage. Low, mounded plants grow 10 inches high and spread to 18 inches. Hundreds of dainty single blossoms brighten each plant. Available in gold and yellow.

Center marigold is red and gold hybrid. Small French marigold (left) is one parent; African is the other.

'Climax' is one of the most popular of the tall Africans. Vigorous, uniform growth; prolific bloom.

MARIGOLDS 39

All-Time Favorites:

NASTURTIUMS

Don't underestimate the value of nasturtiums in your garden. These colorful, easy growing annuals, often considered a bit commonplace or old-fashioned, are capable of doing effective landscape jobs. Few plants oblige with such quick cover for a new garden, or fill a plant box with such vivid splashes of color. They bloom from early summer until frost.

You can get plants with single, semi-double, or double flowers in shades of yellow, orange, salmon, rose, and red. Seed is available in straight colors or in packets of mixed colors.

Perhaps the outstanding plus factor of nasturtiums is their versatility. Dwarf forms make fairly compact mounds only a foot high for borders and pots. You can use the semi-tall varieties as a ground cover on a

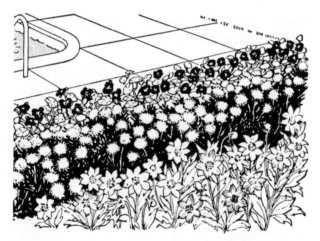

Double row of red and yellow nasturtiums serves as edging for medium-height yellow marigolds, dwarf dahlias.

flat area or as a fast bank cover. Creeping and tall forms are made to order for a temporary fence cover until more permanent plant material can take over (they must have support, such as wire mesh or chicken wire, if they are to climb).

Owners of cabins and vacation houses can count on flowers with little or no work by scattering a packet or two of nasturtium seeds on sunny, cleared ground. Once they get a start, nasturtiums persist without becoming a nuisance, and they don't look out of place growing among natives.

Nasturtium leaves, borne in abundance, are invaluable for softening the appearance of trafficways around house.

For a handsome display of trailing nasturtiums, grow them on a wire mesh triangular frame in a container on the patio; this makes an eye-pleasing pyramid. In winter, pull the nasturtiums off the frame and move the container out of sight until it is time to reseed in spring.

A bed of nasturtiums will crowd out most weeds; if a weed does get a foothold, the nasturtiums just clamber up over it and shade it out.

Hummingbirds love to dip their long bills into nasturtium flowers, so plant a few where you can watch from a window.

Culture

Plant nasturtium seeds where you want them to grow, in pots or in the garden. (It is best not to start them in flats because they are difficult to transplant.) Set the seeds 1/2 to 1 inch deep, and firm them in. Set 4 to 6 seeds to a 6-inch pot, then thin out so you end up with 3 plants. Set the seeds about 10 inches apart if you grow them in rows. On large areas where individual seeding is impossible, work the soil first, then broadcast the seed and lightly rake it in.

Children love to plant nasturtiums; seeds are easy to handle, light colored enough to see against dark ground.

Trailing nasturtiums can't cling to a surface, but they will twine happily about wire or an open block wall.

Nasturtiums bloom best in full sun and in medium to dry soil that isn't too rich. In part shade they put on good foliage growth, but tend to be a little bloom-shy. Some gardeners grow nasturtiums just for their foliage.

In most sections of the country, nasturtiums begin to die off in a hurry with the arrival of autumn's first cold snap, and you have to yank them out. However, in very mild-winter areas, they may live over like perennials and they also seed themselves.

Beware of Aphids

Nasturtiums are susceptible to heavy infestations of aphids, which cluster on the undersides of the big round leaves and on tender new growing tips. Spray with a good general purpose insecticide; be sure to combine it with a spreader or sticker, because nasturtium leaves shed liquid like waxed paper.

Good Cut Flowers

Garden nasturtiums are old-time cut flowers with a pungent fragrance and a reputation for keeping extremely well. If long, trailing stems are brought indoors before frost and placed in bowls or vases on window sills, they will form roots and grow all winter long. Flowers and leaves of nasturtium in bean pots or pottery bowls are among the easiest and most cheerful of arrangements you can make.

Varieties

'Gem Mixture' is the best compact, double-flowered nasturtium for edgings and for small beds. It stays low (10 to 12 inches) and comes in many shades of pink, apricot, salmon, and mahogany.

'Gleam' has slightly larger, spreading plants, and fully double flowers up to 2½ inches across. It comes in straight colors or mixed. 'Scarlet Gleam' and 'Golden Gleam' are bright, showy colors; both are All-Americas.

Double flowers of 'Cherry Rose' are held up above the foliage, a habit unique among nasturtiums.

Tall forms are available in mixed colors, including bicolors. They are effective as trailing plants or as climbers. Blossoms are semi-double or single; plants are robust, with long runners.

All-Time Favorites:
PANSIES AND VIOLAS

Flowers of 'Felix', a novelty pansy, look like cat faces; black "whiskers" are penciled across yellow faces.

Ask a beginning gardener if he knows the difference between a pansy and a viola, and chances are that he won't know. Here is a brief description of the differences between the two:

A pansy is just one of many members of the violet family. Pansies *(Viola tricolor hortensis)* come in mixes and in separate colors of rich blue, gold, red, and white. Petals are usually striped or blotched, and the flowers look like little faces. Plants are compact, seldom exceeding 8 inches in height.

Violas *(V. cornuta)* come in solid colors—blue, yellow, apricot, ruby, and white. Their flowers are usually smaller than those of pansies; also, violas form more tufted, mounding plants than do pansies.

Differences in culture are so minor as to be inconsequential. Although we refer mainly to pansies in the discussion below, the same information applies for violas.

In the true sense, pansies are perennials. But, being short-lived, they are treated as annuals; and, as annuals, their season extends from July (when seed is sown) to the following June or thereabouts. Spring is their time of glory, and whether you start your own plants from seed or buy nursery transplants, everything must be timed so plants can be set out as soon as possible after danger of heavy frost has passed. (Pansies are hardy and will tolerate light frosts.)

In cool regions, pansies can bloom right through summer if flowers are picked regularly and a rigid watering schedule is followed. In hot areas, they are pulled out in June or July.

Pansies are invaluable as edgings, as fillers in perennial borders, and as an accompaniment to spring bulbs. Because they thrive in semi-shade, they make excellent temporary ground covers under flowering shrubs and trees. They are favorite subjects for window boxes, and are also grown in pots and other containers.

Starting From Seed

Pansies transplant easily, and most gardeners buy or grow them in flats for spring bloom. If you grow them yourself, follow the flat-planting procedure described on page 7.

In cold-winter areas, pansies are frequently started from seed in greenhouses or coldframes in midwinter. If you live in an area where winters are mild, you will be well rewarded if you start seed in July or August; you will get some bloom in the fall, maybe a little in winter, and full-fledged, all-out performance throughout the entire spring.

Seeds will germinate in 10 to 15 days. When they have grown two sets of true leaves, prick them out and plant them 3 inches apart in a second flat. Water them with a solution of liquid fertilizer every 2 weeks.

Planting Out

When plants are 2 to 3 inches tall, they are ready to be set out. Set the flat outdoors for a week to "harden" plants (accustom them to cold). If frosts are present at this time, spread a loose mulch of peat moss or leaf mold over the flat so the frost will not uproot the young plants. If weather remains cold or rainy, it is all right to delay planting out; pansies transplant quite easily even when they are in bloom.

To grow compact, free-blooming pansies, plant them in an area with at least full morning sun in a crumbly, loamy soil enriched with well rotted manure, rich compost, or complete fertilizer. Soil should be well drained, yet capable of retaining moisture; dig in a 1-inch layer of peat moss or ground fir bark if your soil is inclined to cake.

If you want a massed or ground cover effect, space pansies 8 inches apart. Always set them at the same depth as they were in the flat. If planted too shallowly, they produce weak stems; when planted too deeply, the plants become stunted.

Always water plants in flats thoroughly one day prior to transplanting. Many gardeners make the mistake of blocking out plants from flats in which the soil has become hard and compact. When the plant is set in the ground, water flows *around* the soil block instead of *through* it, and the fine roots suffer from drought. If soil in the flat remains hard, even after watering, break up the root ball of each blocked-out plant by crushing it gently in your hand before you set it in the ground. Roots will then receive water and make their way into the surrounding soil.

Water after planting, being careful to see that the fine roots are covered. Keep pansy roots cool in summer with a light, moisture-retentive mulch of peat moss, leaf mold, or well rotted manure (processed steer manure is readily available).

Following Through

Let's consider a few things you can do to help these lovable plants grow their best:

Feed generously. Pansies perform best if they are fertilized regularly. Diluted doses of liquid fertilizer applied every 3 or 4 weeks will give excellent results.

Water thoroughly. Never let pansies dry out. In addition to soaking the ground at regular intervals, shower them often with a light mist spray from the hose.

Keep the ground loose. If you cultivate, be careful not to injure roots by working too close to them with a sharp tool. Safer than cultivating is mulching with peat moss, fir bark, or any other form of humus.

Pinch and pick. Pinch pansies if they are leggy. Keep blooms picked off until plants are established. If plants are bushy and producing plenty of sideshoots, further pinching is unnecessary. Once they are in full bloom, pick as often as you can.

Control pests. Don't let aphids take hold; they stunt the plants, yellow the leaves, and deform the flowers. Spray early with a good contact-type insecticide. Baits will control snails and slugs. Some birds love to eat pansies, especially young plants. You can, of course, cover the plants with wire; however, you can prevent much of this sort of thing if you grow pansies in nursery rows or pots until they are big enough to hold their own in the garden. If you have quail, deer, or rabbits in your area, better forget about pansies; they love to feast on the entire plant— down to, and sometimes including, the roots.

Good Cut Flowers

Pansies and violas are attractive in small spring arrangements with grape hyacinths, scillas, small daffodils, primroses, cyclamen, and other spring flowers. It is best to cut long stems, with buds and leaves, rather than flowers alone. They will keep for 3 or 4 days in deep water, although it may be necessary to remove faded blooms from time to time.

Varieties

Varieties of the Swiss Giant strain of pansies are popular favorites, with large flowers. They are available in several straight colors, in bicolors, or in a mixed assortment. Arcadia Mixed, another popular giant-flowered type, is available in a mixture of pastel colors.

Among the good viola varieties are 'Blue Perfection' (light blue) and 'Arkwright Ruby' (dark red).

Violas and alyssum go well together. Set out plants of both, or sow alyssum seed between plants of violas.

DARROW M. WATT

All-Time Favorites:

PETUNIAS

There was a time, not too many years ago, when the petunia was considered to be a rather unimpressive, single flower on a spindly, leggy plant. Then the plant breeders began making one exciting discovery after another, and the ugly duckling days came to a crashing halt. Petunias became more compact and free-flowering. Today petunias rank with marigolds and zinnias at the very top of the home gardener's list of summer blooming annuals.

Because petunias thrive in almost all temperate climates, they have a big advantage over many other annuals, which have a more limited adaptation. Petunias are favorites all over the world, and home gardeners are always eager for new varieties. Hybridists have met the demand successfully. Today there are hundreds of top-notch varieties, and a petunia almost always appears among winners of All-America awards. Colors range from soft pink to deepest velvety-red, silver-blue to richest purple, and pure white to cream. There are also bicolors.

For a clean, nautical effect, plant white petunias in front of dark blue asters, such as Crego Blue.

Petunias are a landscape favorite, and are second to none as an edging and border plant. They combine well with other plants, or they can be very effective in mass plantings by themselves. Many varieties do well in pots and containers.

Culture

Petunias are easily grown from seed sown in flats or in open ground, following the procedures described in the first chapter. Seeds are tiny and should be mixed with fine sand before sowing to insure even distribution. Germination takes about 10 to 12 days.

Pots of white 'La Paloma' petunias add a cheerful note of welcome to a handsome brick courtyard entrance.

Petunia 'Fire Chief' (All-America) is a rich red. Try it with gray plants and edging of white sweet alyssum.

BEN J. ALLEN

Petunias in white and cream colors are versatile as heavy-duty landscaping plants. They combine naturally and *easily with shrubs, as evidenced by this interplanting on a sunny terrace. They won't clash with flowering shrubs.*

In regions where summers are short, sow seed in flats, 10 weeks prior to the frost-free date. Prick them out into flats or individually into pots or bands, and set them out when frosts are over and soil has started to warm up.

In some mild climate areas, petunias can be sown outdoors any time of year; generally, however, spring is the best time.

Petunias take a little longer from seed-to-flower than some other popular annuals, and they are somewhat tricky to handle in the early stages. For these reasons, many gardeners prefer to buy young plants at a nursery. Insist on young, sturdy seedlings; avoid leggy, woody, half-grown plants—they will give you little if any satisfaction.

Plants should be spaced about 8 to 18 inches apart, depending on the variety you are growing. A location in full sun gives the best results, but they will also perform quite satisfactorily in partial shade. Any good garden soil will do; single-flowered types will thrive even in the poorest soil. Gardeners in the low desert regions of the West consider petunias to be

their most rewarding winter and spring annual. They luxuriate in low desert soil and climate from October to late April or May. Petunias are one of the few flowers that will take the dry heat and wind of the southern Great Plains.

Frilled, trumpet-shaped white petunias add zest to a mass planting of shrubs in a curved raised bed.

ART HUPY

Once they are established, petunias require little fussing over. They do not require large amounts of water. For maximum performance, give them an occasional fertilizing. When young plants are 6 inches high, pinch them back to promote side branching. If plants begin to look tired and bloomed-out in midsummer, cut them back to about 6 inches from the ground, follow with a fertilizing and a thorough soaking, and then don't look at them for awhile. In a week or two they'll be coming back strong.

Petunias are seldom bothered by pests. They are relatively disease-free, although in humid areas botrytis spots and eventually ruins blossoms. Botrytis is very difficult to control. If you are troubled with it, plant a botrytis-resistant variety.

Use in Arrangements
Cut petunias last for several days if you pick off the untidy faded blooms regularly. The singles keep better than the large double forms. Most effective arrangements use petunias in masses of one color or two harmonizing colors, such as white petunias in a white bowl, or lavender and purple petunias in a silver bowl. Petunias and annual phlox in harmonizing shades combine beautifully.

Kinds and Varieties
F₁ Hybrid Grandiflora: These vigorous plants grow to 15 inches high and spread to 24 inches; some varieties have fringed flowers. Flowers are large — to 4½ inches on some varieties. No other petunias beat the Grandifloras for mass color effect. Single-flowered varieties include 'Blue Lace', light blue laced with deep violet, deeply fringed and ruffled; 'Calypso', red and white variegated, fringed; and 'La Paloma', white, fringed. Double-flowered types are lovely without question, but plants are a bit weak and hard to start, and old

Celosia grows as easily as petunias, likes same conditions. Combine them for a happy-go-lucky summer border.

'Snowstorm' petunias and nierembergia 'Purple Robe' make a delightful combination in a sunny border.

blossoms hang on after drying up. 'Victorious' is a popular variety, available in straight or mixed colors.

F₁ Hybrid Multiflora: This type grows to about the same size as the F₁ Grandifloras, but flowers are generally smooth-edged and smaller, to 2¾ inches across. Resistant to botrytis disease. Because growth is neat and controlled, these are ideal for mass plantings. 'Comanche' (red) and 'Coral Satin' (coral rose) are two All-America varieties. 'Sugar Plum' (orchid) is another popular favorite.

F₂ Hybrids: Like the F₁ classes, these are also available in Grandiflora and Multiflora types. A good Grandiflora variety: 'Carnival', with variegated flowers in a mixture of white and reddish pink. Multifloras include 'Colorama' and 'Confetti' (both are available in mixed colors).

Fringed Grandifloras: These vigorous plants grow up to 16 inches high and bear fringed, frilled, and ruffled flowers up to 4 inches across. Of variable habit, they are useful in pots and planters, and as interplants in shrub borders; they are not for bedding. Old favorites include 'Fringed Snowstorm' (white) and 'Theodosia' (rose).

Smooth-Edged Grandifloras: These have the same growing habit and flower size as the Fringed Grandifloras. Popular varieties are 'Bingo' (wine-red and

It takes only one or two dozen petunias, with their spreading growth habit, to brighten a circular raised bed.

Tub planting of colorful petunias makes good base and ballast for a patio umbrella. Note handle on planter.

white), 'Dazzler' (carmine), 'Popcorn' (white), and 'Purple Prince'.

Dwarf Giants of California: This group is among the largest flowering petunias. Heavily ruffled and with veined throats, the blooms average 5-6 inches across. Colors include salmon, deep rose, wine-red, magenta, orchid, and white. Their real place is in containers and raised beds, but they are sometimes grown effectively in masses. Good variety: 'Ramona' (dark shades, light shades, mixed).

All-Doubles: These were the first F_1 hybrid petunias. Although the plants are not as free-flowering as the other types, they more than justify their high cost with frilled and ruffled blooms of exquisite beauty. When planting mixtures, intermix equally the larger and smaller sized seedlings because they probably represent different colors. Use All-Doubles in pots, planters, window boxes, or hanging baskets. 'Victorious' (All-America) is available in a mixture of purple, orchid, white, and pink.

Petunia 'Super Frills' has deeply frilled petals giving appearance of double flowers. Plants are lanky.

'Satellite' petunia is bright rose with a white star. Bed of them can brighten an area between lawn, evergreens.

All-Time Favorites:

SCARLET SAGE

Flower-laden spikes rise well above scarlet sage's dark green foliage. Bracts (floral leaves) are also colored.

If you like the brightest of reds, scarlet sage should be one of your favorite flowers. It will liven up a garden from midsummer right on through late fall.

Tubular flowers are a dazzling, strong scarlet including the colored flower bracts, arranged in terminal spikes that rise well above the dark green foliage. Height may be 1 to 3 feet, depending on variety.

Scarlet sage's blazing color can be a detriment if it is misused. It will overpower other colors, particularly soft pastel shades. To see that it gets its just due, let's consider ways to take best advantage of its shrublike form and color, with some uses other than the usual one—as a bedding plant.

Scarlet sage is at its best where its blazing red flowers can stand out against a dark background.

Ways to Use

Tuck a few plants of dwarf scarlet sage among rocks on a bank, particularly in a spring blooming rock garden where midsummer green needs a spicing of scarlet.

There is nothing like silver gray foliage to point up the brilliant color. Highlight a small clump of scarlet sage against a light gray mass of *Artemisia* 'Silver King' or dusty miller. If you like sparkling colors, plant in combination with white petunias and verbena. Or, if you'd prefer to tone down the intense

color, try it against a background of broad leafed evergreens.

Culture

Scarlet sage takes longer to grow than most annuals; therefore, it is best to start seeds indoors in February or March, in flats placed where they can get direct sunlight and air and can be kept at a temperature of 65° to 70°. When the seedlings have developed their first true leaves, transplant about 2 inches apart into other flats. Set them out 18 inches apart in a sunny place when the soil warms.

If you aren't much of a seed gardener, you'll find the young plants in good supply at most nurseries in the spring.

A moderately rich, well drained soil is ideal, although scarlet sage often performs admirably in soil that leans toward the poor side. Be sure to give it plenty of water.

Despite its sturdy appearance and performance in the garden, scarlet sage does not qualify as a longlasting cut flower; the blooms start dropping from the spikes soon after they are arranged.

Good Varieties

'St. John's Fire', an excellent dwarf variety, grows to 12 inches high. 'Bonfire' is a good medium size, reaching 2 to 3 feet in height.

All-Time Favorites:

SNAPDRAGONS

Tall stately snapdragons are among the most beloved of garden flowers. At their feet are violas in mixed colors.

The snapdragon is one of those familiar flowers that always warms our hearts when we see it in a garden. The reason may be the warmth of its colors, or the abundance and velvety texture of its flowers, or perhaps a childhood memory of the fun of snapping the "dragon's jaws."

This perennial favorite has been improved a great deal over the years. Today's "snaps" have all the charm and beauty of the older ones plus greater vigor and disease resistance, more and larger flowers, and a wider range of colors. Whereas snaps first gained their fame as a hardy cool-season plant, there are varieties today that will take considerably more heat than

Snapdragons, not famed for their foliage, are enhanced in this arrangement by large, handsome loquat leaves.

the older strains and grow right through summer in cool climates. Most important single improvement has been the development of varieties that resist rust, the foliage-destroying nemesis. Also important has been development of the double flowered type.

Ways to Use Snapdragons

These garden favorites add a much needed vertical form to the spring garden, and they continue to bloom during summer. They come in just about any color you can think of except true blue.

Taller types are extremely effective in wide borders —they are beautiful with delphiniums, Madonna lilies, and Floribunda roses. They can also be used in small gardens for tall accents here and there. As cut flowers, they are magnificent. Medium-height types are especially well adapted to small gardens; they are excellent bedding plants. Dwarf types are good choices for rock gardens, raised beds, and pots.

Culture

Most gardeners sow snapdragon seeds in flats indoors during the late fall and winter, timing their seed-starting so they will be setting out young plants early in the spring.

You can, if you wish, start seed outdoors in early spring (also in fall, in mild-winter regions). The seeds are very tiny and should be just barely covered with fine soil; this means you may have to water frequently with a fine spray during the 10-day to 2-week germination period in order to make sure that the seeds don't dry out in a thin upper crust of caked soil.

If you're the impatient type, or if you only need a few snaps, you will find young plants to be in good supply at nurseries during the spring months. Avoid young plants that are weak and spindly, or show premature flowers. Chances are, these won't develop into the sturdy, healthy plants you expect.

Plant snapdragons in a sunny location for best results, although they will also get along where they receive sun only half the day. Space tall kinds 18 inches apart, bedding types 10 inches apart, and the very miniature varieties 6 inches apart. Soil should be moderately rich and well drained. Give them plenty of water.

Although it is not an absolute necessity, many gardeners stake snapdragons from the time they are young plants. Staking is a particularly wise idea if you live in a windy area.

It is customary to pinch snapdragons after transplanting to promote base branching. However, this means sacrificing the early central flower spike. Usually, snaps will branch naturally without pinching.

Four of the All-America Rocket series (l. to r.): 'Red Rocket', 'Golden Rocket', 'Rose Rocket', 'White Rocket.'

Tetra snapdragon (right) is far superior to old diploid (left). Note the fuller spike and the larger flowers.

It comes down to this choice; pinch out leaf-stem tips regularly to make bushy plants with short flower spikes; or leave them alone to get fewer, but taller, flower spikes.

For maximum blooming season, it is important to cut flowers frequently and remove faded flowers. When snaps begin to look tired and bloomed-out, cut them back fairly drastically and give them a feeding with fast-acting liquid fertilizer. They will soon be in bloom again. In mild-winter climate areas, they will live through winter and bloom again the following year.

How to Combat Rust

Rust is the snapdragon's most serious disease. You can easily recognize it by the dusty, dark brown spots that appear on the underside of the leaves and on the stem. These brown spots usually appear about the time the flower spikes are developing.

The disease can develop with devastating swiftness; plants in their prime are reduced to a shrivelled study in brown. Typically, if rust is present in a minor degree at the end of one season, a major attack will develop the next. Rust-resistant varieties have been introduced and are usually available; if rust is prevalent in your area, grow them.

To inhibit the disease, dust every 2 weeks with sulfur, starting early in the season, or spray with a fungicide such as parzate. Also, avoid getting leaves wet; apply water at the base of the plants rather than by overhead sprinkling.

This border is all in pastels. Rocket snapdragons comprise over half of 4-foot-wide strip; colors are mainly *pink, rose, and yellow. Billowy salmon pink petunias grow along edge. At the end is fluffy white baby's breath.*

Outstanding Cut Flowers

Snapdragons are splendid cut flowers, lasting about a week. Buds continue to open from the bottom to the top of the spike. They combine well with many flowers, including delphinium, bachelor buttons, bedding dahlias, gladiolus, baby's breath, and roses.

Types and Varieties

Standard (diploid): Plants grow from 18 inches to 4 feet tall. Available in a wide range of colors, in color mixes, and by named variety.

Tetraploid: This class of snapdragons was developed in the late 1940's; the drug, colchicine, was used to increase the number of chromosomes in the cells from 2 to 4. Tetras are stockier plants than the diploids; they have thicker stems, richer green foliage, and larger, brighter colored, more abundant flowers —some with ruffled petals. They are available in straight colors or mixed.

Super Tetras: Introduced in 1962, these are huskier plants than the Tetras, and have large flowers. Well branched from the base, they grow to 2 feet high. Flower colors are crimson, rose, orange, yellow, and white.

F_1 *Hybrids:* These are stronger, more vigorous and have fuller, longer spikes than any other type. They have a greater resistance to adverse weather. Rocket series (All-America) comes in red, rose, orchid, bronze, gold, white, or in a color mixture.

F_2 *Class:* Stronger and better than the old diploids, but not quite as uniform as the F_1 Hybrids. Available in straight colors or mixtures. Panorama and First Ladies are two good series.

Dwarf: Plants grow 4-6 inches high. Magic Carpet is a popular color mixture.

All-Time Favorites:

STOCK

Stock has been a popular favorite with American gardeners ever since the days of George Washington, when this hardy cool season annual was known as the gilliflower. Since that time new forms have been developed, and today it is a greater favorite than ever before. One may now have stock in tall or lower forms. The color range has been widened; you can find them in shades of pink, lavender, purple, yellow, red (mostly darker hues—there is no clear red), and white.

There are two big reasons why stock continues to hold its place as one of the front-running annuals year after year: 1) It has a unique, spicy fragrance that can perfume an entire garden; and 2) it is a splendid cut flower.

On the debit side of the ledger, it is true that stock does not always measure up to some of the other annuals as a garden subject. However, a well-grown bed of stocks can be quite pleasing to even the most discerning eye—provided that they are properly situated. They are effective in mass plantings.

Trysomic Seven Weeks has compact spikes; produces a higher percentage of doubles from seed than other stock.

APLIN-DUDLEY STUDIOS

Climate Is Important

What types of stock you should grow depends on where you live. The Giant Imperial and Column types, tall-growing (2 feet) and spectacular as cut flowers, are recommended only for areas with mild winters. Sow seed outdoors directly where you want them to grow; the long winter vegetative period will prepare them for spring bloom.

Dwarf Ten Weeks and Trysomic Seven Weeks types can be grown successfully in either mild or cold climates. The best way to grow them is to seed very early (at sweet pea time) in spring, outdoors. Sow the seeds thickly; later on, do not thin or feed the young plants. This forces an early blooming period, and they will stay in bloom until early July.

Avoid Sudden Check

Any interruption of growth can have serious consequences. If you sow seed in flats, be sure to set out the young plants before they become flatbound. (Stocks are a popular item in nurseries; you'll do best if you shop for them early.)

A sunny location is best, but light shade is acceptable in hot climates. Soil should be light, fertile, and —above all—well drained. Stocks should be watered regularly, but stems will rot if water is allowed to collect in pools at the base of the plants. If you have heavy soil, you'll get best results by planting on ridges or in raised beds.

If caked soil necessitates light cultivating, proceed with caution so you will not disturb the roots.

Don't hesitate to pull up the occasional unwanted single-flowered plants which invariably crop up in any planting of stock.

Use in Arrangements

Stocks are favorites for cutting, and will keep indoors from several days to a week. Blooms are beautiful in big bowls by themselves, or combined with carnations, Dutch and German iris, peonies, snapdragons, baby gladiolus, and tulips. Bruising the ends of the stems before arranging helps to increase water intake and life of the cut blooms.

Types and Colors

Column, Giant Imperial, and Dwarf Ten Weeks types are available in straight colors (described above) and mixtures. Trysomic Seven Weeks is available in mixed colors only; seeds are expensive but have a higher percentage of double flowers than other types.

All-Time Favorites:

SWEET PEAS

These hardy climbing annuals have been a favorite with gardeners ever since they were first brought out of their native Sicily nearly 300 years ago.

Their popularity is readily understandable when you consider some of the outstanding characteristics: You can get them in any color, in almost any shade you can think of. Flowers are attractive, delightfully fragrant, and superb for cutting. They bloom in great profusion during the spring and well into summer.

Sweet peas are grown to gather by the basketful, fresh, dainty, fragrant, and long-stemmed—for use as cut flowers. Everything you do in growing them is directed to perfection of the individual flower rather than to a mass of color in the garden. The difference in flowers from carefully tended vines, as opposed to carelessly tended ones, is reward enough for taking pains.

Culture

If you live in a region where winters are mild, you can sow seeds outdoors in late summer for early winter flowering, or in early winter for early spring flowering. (Sweet peas will take moderately heavy frosts.)

In cold-winter areas, sow seed outdoors as soon as you can in early spring, when the ground is dry enough to be worked. Or, if you prefer, start seed

Big selling point for the Multiflora sweet pea (available in mixed colors) is that it bears more flowers per stem.

indoors in bands or peat pots, 6 to 8 weeks prior to the average date of the last killing frost.

Soil for sweet peas should be well drained and rich in nutrients and humus. Prepare for a deep root run by digging a trench at least 18 inches deep. Mix in some steer manure or other humous material with your soil before you shovel it back in, and add a balanced commercial fertilizer to the top 6 inches.

To hasten germination, soak the seeds for a few hours before planting. It is a good idea to treat the seed with a fungicide to protect young seedlings from disease. Sow seeds an inch apart and an inch deep, in single or double rows; cover them with finely sifted soil, tamp it down firmly, and water. Seed will germinate in 5 to 10 days, depending on weather and soil conditions. Don't let them dry out. When the young plants are 4 to 5 inches high, thin them to not less than 6 inches apart.

Although it is not absolutely essential, many gardeners like to plant sweet pea seeds in shallow, 2-inch-deep trenches, 6 inches wide. The trenches act as

Sweet peas climb on twine that runs between ½ by ½-inch crosspiece (bottom of fence) to thumbtacks (at top).

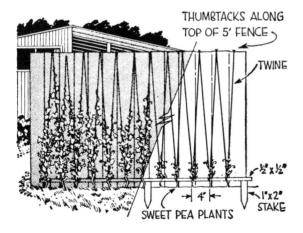

THUMBTACKS ALONG
TOP OF 5' FENCE
TWINE
½"x½"
4"
1"x2"
STAKE
SWEET PEA PLANTS

water-holding basins, keeping the seeds from drying out too fast.

Give sweet peas a sunny location, preferably with an eastern or southern exposure. They should be protected from strong winds. Place a screen over the tender young plants to protect them from birds, and set out bait for slugs and snails.

Sweet peas grow to 5 or 6 feet, and unless you provide some sort of trellis you won't get much of a showing. It is important that this be done right at the beginning, so the vine can find supports as soon as the first tendril is formed. Sweet pea netting is available in many stores; or, train on supporting strands of coarse string 6 inches apart. In some regions you can use chicken wire, but if you live in a desert area or other warm region it is best not to—the wire may become so hot that it will "cook" the vines.

Be sure to give the vines plenty of air space; keep the trellis or wire out from the wall or fence. Best results come from free-standing supports.

Regular watering is vital for sweet peas; give them a deep soaking every week or so, rather than follow the unsatisfactory daily sprinkle method.

Sow seeds in single or double rows, an inch deep and an inch apart, within a 2-inch-deep trench. Don't overwater.

When seedlings are about 5 inches high, pinch out tops to encourage growth of strong side branches at the base.

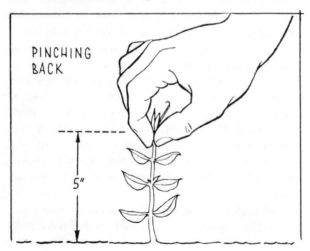

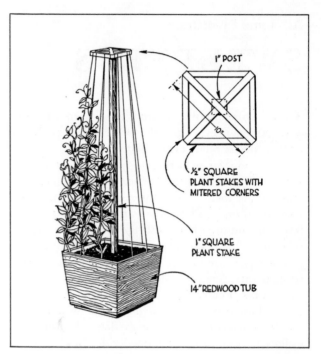

Keep this tub of sweet peas in a narrow entry or at one corner of a patio where flowers are handy for picking.

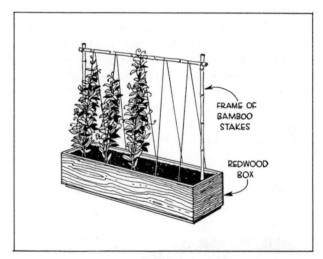

Framework can easily be added to a redwood or cedar plant box to form a divider or screen of sweet peas.

During active growth of the plants, apply a top-dressing that is low in nitrogen but high in potash and phosphates. Sweet peas are legumes (they get their nitrogen supply through the activity of nitrogen-fixing bacteria in the nodules on their roots); the addition of too much extra nitrogen will cause coarse, soft growth and make the plants more susceptible to mildew and virus disease.

Sweet peas provide a sheet of color on south wall, where there's lots of sun plus protection from wind. Problem *of brick wall, which didn't provide a toehold for twining vines, was easily solved (see photograph below).*

Cut the Flowers Frequently

The surest way to miss out on the fun and fascination of sweet peas is to be neglectful in cutting the flowers. For a long and productive blooming season, it is essential to pick flowers every 2 or 3 days and not allow seed pods to ripen.

Sweet peas are outstanding cut flowers, their colorful and fragrant blooms lasting for several days in deep containers filled with cold water. Arrange them in big, loose bouquets, with some of their own leaves and tendrils. Baby's breath adds an airy touch.

Types of Sweet Peas

Cuthbertson Floribunda: A heat-resistant type used mostly for late fall or spring planting.

Early Flowering: Not heat-resistant. Plant these in late summer in mild-winter areas for midwinter bloom.

Multiflora: Spring and early summer flowering. The Galaxy and Zvolanek series are both excellent.

Dwarf: Plants are 8-12 inches high, with a spreading habit. These do well only where summers are cool. 'Little Sweetheart' and 'Color Carpet' are good varieties; both are available in mixed colors.

Sweet pea support in photo at top of page is galvanized 2-inch-square wire mesh stapled to 4 by 4-inch posts.

All-Time Favorites:

ZINNIAS

Year after year, zinnias continue to hold their position as the most popular annual of them all. Let's look at some of the reasons:

A whole garden could be filled with zinnias without fear of monotony. Few flowers can boast as great a diversity; there are hybrids of all sizes, forms, and heights so that these flowers can be used for a variety of planting purposes.

Tall kinds make a strong background for less substantial flowers. Planted in a double row, they act as a friendly property barrier between neighbors. Plants

Yellow and orange Giant Double zinnias soar above buff-yellow annual phlox and edging of matricaria.

in different heights, if kept pinched, have the sturdy value of shrubs in a new garden; as fillers, they can make a newly planted shrub border look full its first year. In a turn-around driveway, massed in selected colors, they extend a warm, bright welcome. The lower-growing kinds are effective for edgings and large-scale ground covers.

The range of colors is extensive—orange, yellow, pink, red, white, purple, and bi-colors. Flowers may be huge or very small, with rays that are flat and papery or twisted into a froth.

Zinnias bloom quickly and easily from seed in about 6 to 8 weeks, depending on variety. They produce quantities of flowers all summer long, and are dependable. Successive sowings in mild climates will produce flowers from early summer to frost. Easy to arrange indoors, they are long lasting as cut flowers.

Culture

These fast growers are naturals for starting from seed outdoors, directly where they are to grow. In spring

JAMES W. WILSON

A row of medium-height zinnias, excellent for cutting, can take away austere appearance of a temporary fence.

or early summer, when the ground has warmed up, plant the seeds in good, well-drained garden soil, in full sun and a warm location. (Some annuals take part shade, but zinnia isn't one of them.) If possible, pick a location that is out in the open where air circulation is good; your zinnias will have a better chance of escaping mildew.

Seeds are large and easy to handle, and will usually germinate in 4 to 6 days. Plant them 4 inches apart and no more than 1/4-inch deep—about 1/8-inch deep if your soil is on the heavy side. Press soil down firmly over the seeds. Be sure not to overwater the seedlings; don't let them dry out, of course, but keep them a little on the "dry side" to discourage damping-off. When plants are 4 inches high, thin them to 8-16 inches apart, depending on what kind you are growing.

Unless transplanted with care, flat-started zinnias will suffer some setback when planted out; be sure to block plants out so as not to expose roots, water in immediately, and provide temporary shade if the weather is warm.

If you buy zinnia transplants at a nursery, look for young ones that have not begun to flower or set buds. (You, the buyer, have something to do with the kinds of plants you get; if you shop *early*, you'll do better.)

When a zinnia has been planted out and has formed its first flower bud, remove the bud in order to develop lateral shoots and thereby encourage better plant form and more flowers later on.

Zinnias like plenty of water. Soak them from below; watering the foliage encourages mildew. Cultivate occasionally, and feed about once a month with a complete commercial fertilizer.

Diseases and Pests

In late summer or early fall when your zinnias are approaching the finale of their bloom period, you may encounter some mildew and you'll wonder: "What—despite my best efforts—happened?" Three "unpredictables" may have caused it. *First,* check your location; is the spot that was so sunny in spring becoming partly shaded now that fall is approaching and the sun's pattern is changing? *Second,* did you really leave enough space between your plants for proper air circulation, or did you squeeze them in a bit too close? *Third,* what kind of weather have you had this summer? Was it cooler than usual? Were there long periods of dark, sunless, rainy days?

Any of the above conditions can bring on mildew. Actually, however, mildew late in the blooming season is almost impossible to avoid consistently. It is a good idea to spray or dust the plants with a fungicide every few weeks while they are young; but if mildew has already appeared, there is little you can do other than to pull and destroy any badly afflicted plants.

Zinnias, like most summer annuals, fall prey to various chewing insects—particularly diabrotica or 12-spotted beetle. Control them with an all-purpose insecticide.

Tiny Cupid zinnias, a foot tall with 1-inch flowers, come in many colors. Try them for cutting, pots, borders.

Outstanding Cut Flowers

All kinds of zinnias, large, medium, and small, make excellent cut flowers that will last 5 or 6 days if properly cared for. Flowers should be well-opened before being cut. Although they can be combined with other summer flowers, such as ageratum, salvia, and gypsophila, they are probably most satisfying by themselves, with their own leaves, or with the substantial

Zinnia 'Blaze' is a tall grower with cactus-like flowers. It is outstanding for cutting (see photo on page 59).

Some of the Giant Double Zinnia varieties have large, broad-petalled flowers that resemble dahlias.

'Persian Carpet' (All-America) is an outstanding small-flowered Mexican zinnia—easy to grow, free blooming.

foliage of shrubs. Remove any zinnia leaves that might contact the water.

Kinds and Varieties

There are many horticultural forms of zinnia, and several new varieties are introduced each year. With-

Lilliput zinnias (this is 'Lilac Gem') are an excellent choice for bedding or borders, come in many colors.

out getting into technicalities, you will have a good working knowledge of what is available if you get to know the following groups of zinnias. Most of them are available in a wide range of colors and varieties; you may also buy seed packets of mixed colors.

Giant Double: Plants 3-3½ feet tall. Large double flowers, 4-5 inches in diameter. Good varieties include 'Enchantress' (pink), 'Isabellina' (cream yellow), and 'Purity' (white). Some varieties have flowers like dahlias; among them are 'Canary Bird' (yellow), 'Golden Dawn' (golden yellow), and 'Scarlet Flame' (scarlet).

Tetra Giant Double: Plants 2-2½ feet tall. Very large flowers, 5-6½ inches in diameter. Good bedding plant. A recent introduction is 'State Fair', available in a wide color range.

Cactus Flowered: Plants 2½-3½ feet tall. Unusual, "shaggy" flowers 4-5 inches in diameter; rays curl upward and are quilled or tubular. Many good varieties and colors. 'Blaze' (All-America), 'Lilac Time', and 'Cherry Time' have colors like their names. 'Trail Blazer', an F_1 hybrid, is a very vivid red. Cactus Mixed has a good range of pastels.

Cut-and-Come-Again (Z. elegans 'Pumila'): Plants grow 18-24 inches high. Stems are long and this is an outstanding zinnia for cutting. Flowers are 2½-3½ inches across; they are smaller than the giant types but there are more of them. Many good varieties and colors. 'Salmon Rose' is a deep, luminous salmon pink. 'Peppermint Stick' has flower rays striped in various bright color combinations.

Mexican: This is *Z. angustifolia,* usually sold in the trade as *Z. haageana.* Mexican zinnias have been bedding favorites for many years. Plants are 12-15 inches high. Flowers range from single to semi-double to double. Blooms are small—seldom more than 1½ inches across—but the stems are long and there is no better garden "cutter" for small bouquets. Good varieties: 'Persian Carpet Mixed' and 'Old Mexico' (both All-Americas); flowers of the latter are bi-colored (mostly yellow and red), and 2-2½ inches across— larger than most of the other varieties.

Lilliput: Plants are 15-18 inches high, compact, and freely branched. Good for mass bedding or low borders. Small double flowers, about 2-2½ inches across. Many excellent varieties; choose the one that best suits your color scheme.

Cupid: Plants seldom more than 12 inches high; very compact. A favorite for edgings. Small double flowers, less than an inch in diameter. Good variety: 'Tiny Tim' (scarlet).

Zinnia 'Peppermint Stick' is a cut-and-come-again type; flower petals are striped with bright colors.

Flowers of Giant Doubles are effective in the garden, but less effective in arrangements than others (see below).

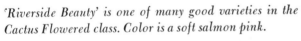

'Riverside Beauty' is one of many good varieties in the Cactus Flowered class. Color is a soft salmon pink.

Zinnia 'Blaze' (All-America) is a favorite for arrangements. Flowers have quilled, twisted, curled petals.

ENCYCLOPEDIA

RARE IS THE GARDENER who has not had the experience of standing in fascinated bewilderment beside a display rack bulging with colorful seed packets, trying to make up his mind what to buy. Like the dedicated bookstore browser, the shopper at the dime store, or the casual scanner of magazine stands, he is temporarily in a sort of limbo.

The information on these pages will help both the seed rack shopper and the gardener who prefers to buy young plants in flats at a nursery.

On pages 32 to 59, we describe a dozen of the best-known annuals. In the following section are 60 additional favorites—some not so well known, but all of them worthy of your consideration. They are listed in alphabetical order, according to the name most commonly found on seed packets and in catalogs. Directly under the common name of each, you will find the proper botanical name, except in cases where the common and botanical names are one and the same. Alternate common names are mentioned in parentheses.

We have placed this chapter at the back of the book for a reason—so that gardeners can flip to it easily and refer to it often. Use it as a guide for deciding which annuals are best suited to your needs and preferences (perhaps you will want to take it along with you the next time you go shopping for annuals). Follow specific cultural directions carefully, and also be sure to review the general planting techniques described in the chapter beginning on page 6.

AFRICAN DAISY

DIMORPHOTHECA (Cape marigold)

Winter and early spring blooming beds of African daisy are a special feature in the mild climate of southwestern low desert areas. They also put on a fine show—a little later, however—in parts of California where winter temperatures generally stay above 25° or 26°. Under these favorable conditions African daisy is so covered with blossoms that the foliage is hardly visible. In more humid areas, spring planted African daisy tends to produce heavy lush foliaged plants with fewer blooms.

Plants grow to·6 to 12 inches high, spreading into solid mounds—useful for planting in parking strips between street and sidewalk, for edging along walks and in flower beds with winter blooming calendulas or violas. African daisies close at night, but last for 2 or 3 days when cut for arrangements.

Broadcast seeds outdoors in late summer so plants will be in bud before cold weather arrives. Plants need full sun. If you live in a cool but dry area where winters are severe, plant seeds outdoors in spring when soil is warm and you will have a good show of blooms from late summer until heavy frost.

Species and varieties: *D. sinuata* (usually sold as *D. aurantiaca*): Daisy-like, 2½-inch white, yellow, apricot, and salmon flowers have a satiny sheen. Plants grow 1 foot high. *D. pluvialis* 'Ringens' (available under the nursery name *D.* 'Hybrida Ringens'): 6 to 8-inch-high plants with very large flowers 4 inches in diameter. One form, Glistening White,' has a blue ring around the blue-black center.

African daisy

AGERATUM

A. HOUSTONIANUM (floss flower)

A choice lavender-blue flowered plant, 8 to 10 inches high in full sun—up to 12 inches high in light shade. Plants spread to 1 foot across and are covered with clustered heads of tiny, silky flowers. Ageratum blooms continuously from early summer until frost, but where summers are long and hot it does best on the east side of the house or in other light shade.

Ageratum 'Midget Blue'
(See color photograph on page 31)

For strong color contrast try blue ageratum as an edging for a bed of ornamental sweet basil 'Dark Opal' or annual Madagascar periwinkle *(Catharanthus)* 'Little Pinkie'. Or, for a quiet feeling, combine with white annual periwinkle 'Little Bright Eye', or blue *Salvia* 'Blue Bedder'.

Gardeners usually start ageratum seeds indoors 8 weeks prior to frost-free date. Seedlings start rather slowly and remain small for quite a while, which pretty well rules out sowing seeds in the garden row. Ageratum produces blooms when plants are very small, and then can be transplanted even after they have started to flower.

Plant ageratum in good, well drained soil, and water regularly. In poor soil, with too little water, the plants turn brown in hot weather; to bring plants back into presentable condition, give them lots of water, feed them once a month, and remove as many dead flower heads as possible. Fresh new ones will develop that will cover the earlier damage.

Varieties: 'Blue Mink', a very dwarf variety with large flower clusters leads in popularity as an edging plant. 'Blue Perfection', a taller variety, has 8 to 10-inch stems which make it a useful filler in the garden as well as in flower arrangements.

ALYSSUM, SWEET

LOBULARIA MARITIMA

(see page 33)

AMARANTHUS

These are big, robust plants that dominate everything around them. One type is grown for foliage, one for flowers, and another for colorful foliage and flowers. Used properly their flamboyant color will attract all who see them—but crowded in with smaller flowering plants they look gaudy and unkempt.

Of the amaranthus with colorful foliage, one or two plants won't do. Try a large bed of them against a tall fence where they can get reflected heat, and watch them grow! Leave plenty of room; each plant spreads to cover 4 square feet, and will reach 4 to 6 feet in height.

Amaranthus should be started where it is to remain. Transplanting stops the growth for weeks. Wait until the soil is quite warm before planting. Feed and water regularly until midsummer, then hold off, especially on those with colorful foliage—they will develop richer colors. Amaranthus occasionally wilts and dies at maturity—usually when you have planted it in the same bed for several years. This failure is due to a root rot disease which is practically impossible to control.

Foliage wilts too quickly to be used in arrangements.

Species and varieties: Most popular is *Amaranthus tricolor* (Joseph's coat), a foliage plant. Don't try to grow this one where summers are cool and short. It would grow slowly and remain a drab color until quite late. Conversely, it is hard to find a garden too hot for it. Its large leaves stay green until midsummer, then become variegated with shades of red and yellow. Even more striking is 'Molten Fire'. Its upper leaves turn flaming crimson, a luminous color visible from a considerable distance. It grows to 1 to 4 feet high.

Amaranthus caudatus

A. caudatus (love-lies-bleeding) is a curious plant with long, red, drooping flower tassels. It grows 3 to 8 feet high. One of its quaint old names is Kiss-me-over-the-garden-gate.

A. hybridus hypochondriacus (prince's feather) is now rarely seen. Years ago it was popular in gardens in the South, but it has largely been replaced by plume celosia, a neater plant. The flowers of prince's feather are in plume-like clusters—they and the leaves vary from maroon to purple, green and gold. Plants grow to 5 feet.

ANAGALLIS

A. LINIFOLIA, usually sold as
A. GRANDIFLORA (pimpernel)

A fine-leafed plant for the rock garden or "wild flower garden" which grows to about 12 inches in height. Although it is a biennial or short-lived perennial, it is usually

Anagallis

grown as an annual. One rarely sees anagallis outside the cool areas of California or in temperate northern or mountain states. It has dainty, gentian-blue blossoms. If it were not for its distinctive blue, there would be little reason for planting it. To get effective color from anagallis it should be planted in generous drifts interspersed with white sweet alyssum, snow-in-summer, or among clumps of dusty miller.

In mild-winter areas you'll get a welcome burst of fresh bloom just before the wet season. Anagallis is not satisfactory for cutting.

Sow seeds in a garden row as soon as soil is dry enough to work in the spring. Seeds are a little slow to start, so cover very lightly. Dig a 1-inch-deep furrow in moist soil; scatter seeds along the furrow and soak the bed, being careful not to wash away the seeds. They'll sprout in 2 or 3 weeks.

ANCHUSA CAPENSIS

(Cape forget-me-not, summer forget-me-not)

How summer gardens need the touch of indigo blue that anchusa provides! In general anchusa is biennial, but the variety 'Blue Bird' is an annual. Plants are vase shaped with many slender, upright branches, 1½ to 2 feet tall.

Sow anchusa outdoors when the soil is warm

Anchusa capensis

and dry. It needs full sun and will mature quickly. Shear the plants after one show of bloom, feed and water, and they will come back with even more color.

Use anchusa in drifts among yellow or pink snapdragons, in beds behind an edging of light yellow dwarf French marigolds, or combine it with *Salvia* 'Blue Bedder' edged with white petunias. Anchusa flowers are too fragile for cutting; they wilt quickly.

ASTER

CALLISTEPHUS CHINENSIS (China aster)

Asters are a standby in gardens whose owners require a steady source of cut flowers all summer long. The 1 to 3-foot-high plants are rather leggy and the long, wiry stems tend to bend under the weight of the heavy 2 to 3-inch-wide flowers. Beds of mixed-color asters are popular; a background of cleome with an edging of sweet alyssum or ageratum frames the plants and sets off the pastel and deeper aster colors—pure white, lavender-blue, lavender, violet, pink, purple, wine, and crimson.

If the frost-free season is less than 5 months,

Aster Crego
(See color photograph on page 31)

start asters indoors 8 weeks prior to the usual date for the last spring frost. Otherwise, plant seed outdoors. Asters have big seeds which sprout quickly. Seedlings transplant with little fuss.

Aster yellows is a serious disease which is unfortunately quite prevalent. Plants turn yellow, then die. Control by keeping a strict preventive program against sucking insects —carriers of the disease.

Aster has few peers as a cut flower; fortunately, keeping faded blossoms trimmed off stimulates new bloom. The long, thin stems are easy to work into arrangements and the flowers will last for a week or more. Arrange in single colors or in harmonious shades such as lavender and purple or soft pink and rose. White asters and gladiolus are handsome together.

Varieties: Powderpuffs. Probably the best

double flowered home garden aster. Upright 2-foot-high, compact plants—each looks like a bouquet. Crested flowers, quilled rays. Many rich colors with some bicolors. Double Crego has shaggy blossoms, 3 inches across, with twisted rays. Plants are 3 feet tall.

BABY-BLUE-EYES

NEMOPHILA MENZIESII, usually sold as N. INSIGNIS

This Western spring blooming native has clear blue 1-inch-wide flowers with white centers. They are borne on short, fragile stems above spreading, rather succulent, leafy plants only 6 to 10 inches high. It is a refreshing color when used in drifts in rock gardens or as an edging for other cool-loving, quick-blooming annuals such as nemesia or linaria, or among tall daffodils.

Seed baby-blue-eyes in fall or very early spring. Scatter thickly because plants are dainty and fine-leafed. It needs moist soil; shade from afternoon sun will prolong the bloom.

Plants trail attractively when used in hanging baskets or window boxes.

In arrangements, group bunches of nemophila blossoms with spring bulbs such as daffodils, scillas, tulips, or in mixed bouquets. Flowers are fragile, but will keep for 2 or 3 days.

Baby-blue-eyes

Baby's breath

BABY'S BREATH

GYPSOPHILA ELEGANS

Baby's breath is unmatched for frothy lightness. Plants grow rapidly to 2 feet, slender criss-crossing stems profusely covered with tiny, rounded, pearly-white blossoms. A plant in full bloom looks like a fluffy white cloud. (There also are pink and rose forms, but they are rarely planted.)

There is little point in preparing special beds for baby's breath. The plants are short lived—lasting only 5 or 6 weeks in summer. For a steady supply of flowers, sow seeds at intervals of 3 to 4 weeks. Rake up old bulb beds, small areas in front of shrubs, unused corners in the vegetable or herb garden. Scatter seeds, rake over lightly to cover, then firm in the seeds by placing a board over the soil and walking over it—or simply walk over the area once or twice. Seeds sprout faster when pressed down into firm contact with the soil. Be sure not to try this on soggy, heavy soil, or it will become as hard as brick.

White baby's breath is invaluable for use as an accent or filler in arrangements, large or small, but particularly in old-fashioned bouquets. You'll use it often as a contrast with large, dark colored flowers which need the balance its lightness provides.

Varieties: 'Covent Garden', white, is widely used. A pink variety is also available, but it is not nearly as adaptable.

BACHELOR BUTTON

CENTAUREA CYANUS (cornflower)

Bachelor buttons come in pink, white, rose, and the newer deep wine colors—boutonniere-size blossoms on 2-foot-high plants. Plants are shaggy, with gray-green foliage and upright stems. The lower leaves are generally unsightly, so an edging such as white annual candytuft or sweet alyssum is called for. Although the rather unkempt plants of bachelor button will take no prizes for beauty, they yield many flowers for cutting before hot weather annuals come into bloom.

Bachelor button is simple to grow; seeds are good size and sprout quickly. Start the plants outdoors in full sun where they are to remain. Except where temperatures drop to 15°-20°, bachelor button should be seeded in late summer or fall—by January at the latest. Plants bloom until July, then burn out. Fall seeded plants thus have weeks of additional bloom. Where winters are severe plant seed outdoors as soon as soil is dry enough to work.

Bachelor button

Varieties: Tall Double comes in mixed colors. 'Tall Blue' is the favorite. Plants have long stems which are good in arrangements. 'Jubilee Gem' is a 12-inch-high edging plant with light blue flowers that are a little smaller than those of the tall variety; its stems are too short for cutting.

BALSAM

(see IMPATIENS)

BELLS OF IRELAND

Molucella laevis (shellflower)

These curious looking flowers are garden oddities, but they make interesting fresh or dried arrangements. Bells of Ireland branches quite low and grows 2 to 3 feet high. The gracefully curving flower stems have many whorls or soft green bell-like

Bells of Ireland

flowers. Actually these bells are the calyx of the flower. The white petals tucked in the center of the bell are inconspicuous.

Bells of Ireland seeds need warmth to sprout. Start seeds indoors at 75° where the summers are short. Elsewhere, seed in sunny, warm soil in early summer, or if summers are quite long and hot, sow seeds in August for fall flowers. Give plants regular applications of plant food and don't let them suffer from drought if you want extra long, full flower stalks.

As cut flowers, fresh or dried, they are long lasting and easy to arrange. Their unusual color and interesting form combines beautifully with snapdragons, gladiolus, chrysanthemums, small dahlias, or zinnias. And they are handsome in arrangements by themselves.

To dry the flower spikes for winter bouquets, cut them when they are in their prime. Remove the leaves because they wilt rapidly. Tie the spikes in clusters and hang them upside down in a cool, well ventilated room to dry. They can also be sprayed with various colors for unusual effects.

BLACK-EYED SUSAN VINE

Thunbergia alata (clockvine)

This dainty twining vine has attractive 1½-inch-wide flowers in orange, yellow, cream,

Black-eyed Susan vine

or white; many have jet black centers. Actually it's a perennial, but usually grown as a summer blooming annual; in mild-winter areas it may live over for more than a year in sheltered locations.

Black-eyed-Susan vine is unusual and easiest to grow in hanging baskets, pots, and planter boxes where its neat short runners can cascade over the sides. However, it can also be trained on low trellises. Tying at intervals will keep it up in areas where heavy summer rains are frequent.

Plant seed outdoors in warm soil in a sunny location. These vines grow rapidly with warmth and moisture. If you grow them in containers, feed them about once a month; leaves of starved plants lose their rich green color.

Varieties: Seeds are generally available only in mixed colors.

BLUE LACE FLOWER

Trachymene caerulea, formerly called Didiscus caerulea

The 1½ to 2-foot-high plants have finely divided leaves. Many small blue flowers are in 2 to 3-inch, umbrella-like clusters surrounded by a lacy green frill. These plants are grown almost solely for flowers because they are too open and uneven for bedding. Plants stay in bloom only a few weeks during late spring.

Blue lace flower

Plant seeds in full sun out of doors in the spring when soil is warm and dry. Seedlings seem to resent transplanting.

The lacy flowers are excellent in flower arrangements and keep for several days. They combine effectively with salmon or white godetia, candytuft, sweet peas, bachelor button, larkspur, and baby's breath.

Blue is the best known color, but white and pink varieties are available from specialty seedsmen.

BROWALLIA

(amethyst flower)

Browallia, although not well known, is a good pot plant for winter and equally good for bedding in sunny, warm gardens. It needs protection from afternoon sun which bleaches leaf and flower colors and stunts plants.

Sow seeds indoors 8 to 10 weeks prior to

Browallia

warm weather. Seeds sprout in 2 weeks at 70° to 75°. Seedlings transplant easily, but don't set them out until all trees are in full leaf. Give plants plenty of fertilizer and water, particularly during hot weather.

Species and varieties: *B. speciosa.* In warm, sheltered locations, plants are large and bushy reaching 2 to 3 feet high; in cool spots they grow to about 12 inches. Single, petunia-like, lavender-blue blossoms with white throat, 2 inches wide.

B. americana 'Sapphire', a dwarf variety, is too small for outdoor use except in sheltered planter boxes or patio tubs. Dark blue flowers, white eye.

BUTTERFLY FLOWER

SCHIZANTHUS PINNATUS (poor man's orchid)

Butterfly flower is very popular in mild-winter areas of California for winter and early spring bloom. It also does well in mountain sections and in northern areas where summer nights are cool. The 1½-foot-high plants have lacy foliage which is nearly hidden under tumbling masses of colorful 1-inch-wide flowers. Blossoms look somewhat like small orchids in soft pink, rose, lilac, purple, and white with vari-colored markings.

In mild-winter areas, start seeds in August for winter bloom. Seeds are slow to germinate. Here is one way to start schizanthus

Butterfly flower

from seed: Fill a plastic refrigerator dish with vermiculite or sphagnum moss, moisten, drain off excess water, and scatter seeds. Cover seeds with 1/16 inch of the planting material and place the planter in a plastic bag. Put planter on a window sill and water it lightly, once a week. Remove bag when first seedlings emerge. In 6 or 8 weeks little plants will be ready to set out. Protect them for 2 or 3 days from the sun and wind with newspaper hoods or with lath shade.

Seeds can be started outdoors if you have a shaded bed with good soil rich in humus such as used for tuberous begonias. Scatter a few seeds, cover lightly, and keep the soil moist. Transplant when seedlings have 4 to 6 leaves. Butterfly flowers do well under filtered shade of high-branching trees and are excellent container plants.

Cut flowers last for 3 or 4 days. Combine with tulips, forget-me-nots, cyclamen, columbine, ferns.

Varieties: Dr. Badger's Mixed contains all the schizanthus colors.

CALENDULA

(pot marigold) See page 35

CALIFORNIA POPPY

ESCHSCHOLZIA CALIFORNICA

This sun loving California native will grow anywhere in light, well drained soil. These poppies are perennials that are usually grown as annuals. They are attractive plants 1 to 2 feet high with blue-green lacy foliage. The petals of the cup-shaped flowers have a satiny sheen. Blossoms close up each night and when they fade they fall off, leaving clean neat plants.

Naturalize California poppies in dry spots along drives, in hard-to-cultivate places

under fences, any place where a spot of cheerful orange-gold is needed to light up summer greenery. They re-seed readily, blooming through spring and into late summer.

Fall or early spring sowing is preferable. Spade beds and leave soil rough; broadcast seeds and let rain wash them into the soil.

If picked while in bud stage and placed immediately in deep, cold water, the flowers will keep for several days. California poppies and blue lupine, often seen growing

California poppy

together in the wild, are effective in arrangements.

Varieties: The native poppy is a glowing orange gold, but seedsmen have developed other colors—pink, creamy white, yellow, and red. Recently the new Mission Bells seed mixture supplies double or semi-double flowers in pink, deep red, scarlet, and yellow. They also may have frilled petals or bicolored flowers.

CALLIOPSIS

COREOPSIS TINCTORIA (annual coreopsis)

This summer blooming annual is one of the easiest flowers to grow. Tall varieties reach 3 feet high and are best used as backgrounds because of their loose, open growth habit. Dwarf calliopsis makes an unusual edging; it grows only 8 to 12 inches high.

Calliopsis has daisy-like flowers; some have golden yellow rays that are reddish brown at the base and brownish purple centers; others are almost solid brown or mahogany. Plant seeds outdoors where plants are to

Calliopsis

remain. Seeds are not harmed by cold and can be sown as early as soil can be worked in the spring. Calliopsis blooms all summer long, except the low growing varieties— they burn out in late summer. Tall calliopsis is very good for cutting.

CANDYTUFT

IBERIS

Globe candytuft *(I. umbellata)* produces mounding 12 to 15-inch plants covered in late spring and early summer with pink, rose, salmon, lilac, or white flowers in tight rounded clusters. When grown in extensive borders or edgings, this annual makes spectacular drifts of pastel colors.

Hyacinth-flowered candytuft *(I. amara),* sometimes called rocket candytuft, carries snowy white flowers in 10 to 15-inch, hyacinth-like spikes, 3 or more on each plant. Blooming in early spring, it combines well with daffodils, Dutch iris, tulips, and other bulbs; it is also effective among winter and early spring flowering heather.

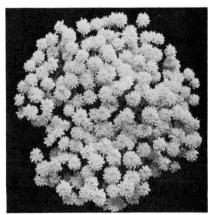

Candytuft

Sow seeds of globe candytuft in late fall or early spring. Since it is somewhat difficult to transplant, it is best to broadcast seed where you want it to grow, although young transplants can be set out successfully. Globe candytuft is adapted to most climates. Hyacinth-flowered candytuft is rarely used outside of mild-winter areas, where it is almost always planted in fall. The early blooming plants are intolerant of heat.

Both kinds of annual candytuft keep for days after cutting. For an easy but effective arrangement, cut an entire plant of globe candytuft at the base and secure it on a needle holder in a low bowl.

CANTERBURY BELLS

(campanula medium)

Canterbury bells are biennials that are planted each year in the same way as annuals. They form sturdy 2½-foot to 4-foot plants with wavy-edged leaves that are 3 to 5 inches long on the upper stems, 6 to 10 inches long at the base. Single or double flowers, shaped like bells or urns, are pink, rose, lavender, violet, and white. A double form, 'Calycanthema', commonly called cup-and-saucer, is available in the same shades.

Canterbury bells

Sow seeds in late spring for plants that will bloom the following spring. Plant in full sun in good garden soil, and water thoroughly during the growing and blooming season. Canterbury bells often re-seed when conditions are favorable.

The strong, heavily flowered stems are excellent for cutting.

CARDINAL CLIMBER

QUAMOCLIT SLOTERI

This free-flowering twining vine is useful for quick temporary screens. The 2 to 4½-inch leaves are dark green and deeply lobed. Morning glory-like flowers are 1½ to 2 inches long, deep red, with white centers. Blossoms remain open except during the hottest part of the day.

Cardinal climber

Plant seeds in full sun where plants are to remain, and where they can climb from 10 to 20 feet. Train them on strings up to the eaves on the sunny side of the house where their light, airy foliage will shade without cutting off the view. Flowers are not durable enough for arrangements.

CELOSIA

(cockscomb)

Use celosia correctly and you can have beds that are breathtaking in their brilliance. Use them haphazardly and your garden will be a hodge-podge of clashing colors; they are so bright they attract attention at once. Plants grow from 6 inches to 3 feet.

Ready to dare? If you'd like bright background flowers, stick to the plume celosia

Celosia (cockscomb)
(See color photograph on page 31)

(*C. argentea*)—large plants with many feathery flower clusters. There are also lovely dwarf forms that make spectacular edgings.

The true cockscombs (*C. argentea* 'Cristata') have velvety flowers arranged in big folded or fan-shaped clusters. The newer kinds are knee high or shorter and best massed in beds.

C. argentea 'Childsii', or Chinese wool-flower, is rarely grown. The plumed heads are tangled into great, loose fluffs.

Although there are gentle colors in celosia (pink, rose, and wine red), if you like brilliant colors try the vivid reds, scarlet, and gold. Watch for good foliage color—maroon or dark green is easier to use in the garden than the chartreuse green of some. Try celosias with white verbena or blue salvia. Occasional groups of celosia among shrubs brighten foundation plantings.

There is little reason to start celosia indoors except where the summers are quite short. Seeds should not be planted outdoors until the soil is warm. Plants grow rapidly in full sun, the hotter the better. Celosia won't tolerate shade.

Flower arrangers dry celosia for winter bouquets. It is one of the few flowers that holds its color when dry. Fresh plumes of celosia combine effectively with marigolds, chrysanthemums, zinnias, or gladiolus.

Varieties: 'Forest Fire', a striking bedding or background plant with orange-scarlet plumes, bronze-red leaves. Good with white petunias in foreground. 'Golden Fleece', soft yellow grading into deep golds, light green foliage. 'Toreador' (All-America), a cockscomb type, 18 inches high, with huge, deep rich red velvety flower clusters.

CHINESE FORGET-ME-NOT

CYNOGLOSSUM AMABILE

A good blue flower where summers are cool. Gray-green foliaged plants 1½ to 2 feet tall are covered with short, dainty clusters of sky blue tiny flowers. Chinese forget-me-not is particularly suited to planting under trees with high shade, among shrubs, and along north and east walls. It combines well with wildflowers, perennial columbine, or impatiens; unfortunately, the delicate flowers wilt quickly after cutting.

Sow seeds outdoors where plants are to remain. Seeds are not harmed by scattering on cold soil in very early spring, and plants will get an early start.

Varieties: 'Firmament' (All-America), is the only widely available variety.

Chinese forget-me-not

CINERARIA

SENECIO CRUENTUS

In the cool shade where cinerarias like to grow, their daisy-like flowers sparkle in light to dark shades of pink, blue, purple, magenta, and shining white during the spring months in California gardens—especially those along the coast. And in these areas it often remains the perennial it is. But many like to grow it as an annual and buy fresh new plants each year. Elsewhere, cineraria is grown as a biennial in greenhouses. Potted plants are often sold in full bloom.

Most gardeners buy cinerarias in flats or pots—usually the large-flowered strains with blossoms in compact large clusters in mixed colors. Plants grow 12 to 15 inches

high, and have attractive, large, heart-shaped leaves. Plants established in the garden often self-sow.

Cinerarias are fairly easy to grow from seed sown in late fall in mild winter areas. Transplant seedlings when they are quite small and they will come into bloom quicker.

For best results grow cinerarias in shaded areas in cool, moist, leafy, well drained soil; poorly drained soil causes root rot. Water them lavishly during their growing period, and on warm days you may have to sprinkle them several times or they will wilt. Plants grown in pots may require frequent feeding—usually every 2 weeks.

ROBERT COX

Cineraria

Leaf miner is cineraria's worst pest. Larvae tunnel the leaves and make plants look unsightly. Once the miner gets inside the leaf it's hard to control, but early preventive spraying with chlordane, malathion, or lindane at 15-day intervals will probably keep it away. The same sprays control aphids, whiteflies, and other pests. You'll also need to bait for slugs and snails in areas where these pests are prevalent.

Cinerarias combine beautifully with other shade loving plants such as ferns and fibrous begonias. They are excellent in pots for color in shady outdoor living areas.

CLARKIA

(mountain garland)

Clarkia, a western native, is rarely grown where summer days average more than 80°. It grows beautifully in Denver, Seattle, and in cool California valleys. Across the northern tier of states it gives a good 6 weeks of summer color before burning out.

Clarkia

ART HUPY

Cleome

In the wild, clarkia usually has single rose pink flowers but most of those in cultivation are double forms of *C. elegans* in mixed colors—orange, salmon, white, cream, yellow, rose, and pink. Plants grow to 2 to 3 feet and have slender ascending branches covered with dainty blossoms tucked in the axils of the leaves.

C. pulchella is lower growing to 12 inches and has reddish stems. Flowers are rose, lilac, pink, or white. This species is not readily available, but some of the garden forms are probably hybrids of *C. elegans* and *C. pulchella*.

Sow seeds outdoors in early spring. Scatter them so clarkia will grow in clumps among taller flowers such as foxglove or hollyhock. Don't water plants unless they are wilting.

Cut branches of clarkia last for several days. Arrange in mixed bouquets with bachelor button, love-in-a-mist, forget-me-not, baby's breath, or Chinese delphinium.

CLEOME

C. SPINOSA (spider flower)

Large, shrub-like plants covered with many open, fluffy flower clusters 1 to 2 feet long. Plants reach 6 feet in warm areas and spread to 4 or 5 feet wide. The airy, rosy pink to white flowers drop soon and are replaced by long, slender seed capsules.

Use cleome for backgrounds, or in large patio tubs. Cleome looks very good against grapestake fences; it can also be grown against solid walls since reflected heat does not faze it. Flower clusters can be used in large arrangements, but old flowers should

be removed daily. Combine with substantial blooms such as gladiolus, pompon or decorative dahlias, or zinnias in pastel shades.

Cleome seed sprouts readily in warm soil outdoors and plants grow rapidly. Only where summers are 4 months long or less should seed be started indoors. Keep plants on the dry side or they will get too rank.

Cleome does well in all 50 states, a claim which can be made for few other flowers.

Varieties: 'Pink Queen' (All-America) is shrimp-pink, 'Helen Campbell' is a pure white variety.

COLEUS

C. BLUMEI

Coleus is a perennial commonly grown as a bedding annual in cold-winter climates. It is probably even better known as a house plant.

It is distinguished principally for its richly colored, toothed, often deeply cut leaves in shades of red, yellow, and purple; beside them the whorls of small dark blue or whitish flowers, held in spikes, are quite insignificant. When grown in strong, indirect light, and given plenty of water and food, coleus plants will reach 3 feet, and their leaves may measure 6 inches across and color vividly. Plants in full sun grow lower, have smaller, less brilliantly colored leaves, and tend to wilt on hot days.

For compact growth and luxuriant foliage, pinch out the growing tips of the plants regularly during summer.

Grow coleus from seed or cuttings. (No two coleus plants grown from seeds will be exactly alike.) Seeds require bottom heat of 70° to 75° for quick germination. Seedlings

grow slowly on short, dull days; as they get more hours of bright light, they put on as much as 2 inches of growth a week.

Cuttings of coleus root easily; simply snap off sideshoots, remove all but the tip leaves, and place them in a glass of water. When they have roots ½ inch or more long, pot them up individually in a mixture of soil, sand, and peat moss or leaf mold. Growing from cuttings is the simplest way to perpetuate your choice varieties, and to be sure of having a supply of plants for growing indoors during the winter.

Aphids and mealybugs commonly attack coleus; control both with lindane or malathion.

Use coleus as a background or filler in arrangements; plain-leafed kinds are preferable in combination with flowers. After cutting coleus, remove the larger leaves at the bottom of the stems, and keep the top ones which will remain firm. Place stems in deep cold water to stiffen them before arranging.

ERNEST BRAUN

Coleus

Varieties: Mixtures, some with very large variegated leaves, include: 'Rainbow', 'Brilliant', and 'Kimono Colors'. Separate colored varieties are: 'Red Velvet', 'Candidum' (green edge on ivory), 'Golden Rainbow' (green flecks on gold), 'Pastel Rainbow' (pale green on pink), and 'Scarlet Rainbow' (scarlet and green).

COSMOS

C. BIPINNATUS

Cosmos blossoms are borne on long pliant stems—up where you can see them—on tall, open, lacy foliaged plants 6 to 8 feet high. Daisy-like flowers are in shades of white, pink, rose, lavender, purple, or crimson, with tufted yellow centers.

Sow seeds outdoors where you want plants

Cosmos
(See color photograph on page 30)

to grow any time from early spring through midsummer. You can also sow in flats and transplant later. Cosmos needs full sun and is best used as a tall background plant or in groups among tall shrubs. Birds will search out your garden as cosmos seeds ripen.

Cut freshly opened cosmos blossoms for arrangements; plunge them immediately in cool water to keep flowers and foliage from wilting. Arrange in loose, airy masses, using plenty of foliage.

Varieties: Early Sensation types: 'Pinkie'—the earliest and brightest pink cosmos. 'Purity'—large white blossoms, combines well with 'Pinkie'. 'Radiance' (All-America) — rosy red and crimson shaded flowers on tall, robust plants. Sensation Mixed Colors contain white, pink, crimson, purple, red, lavender, and rose shades.

DAHLIA, BEDDING

D. MERCKII (dwarf dahlia)

Bedding dahlias are customarily handled as annuals, although tubers, formed during the first growing season, can be planted the following year in the same way as the larger dahlias. The compact, 18-inch-high plants are covered with blooms from midsummer until frost. Double, semi-double, or single flowers, in many rich and glowing colors, are 2 to 3 inches across, held erect on long, slender, rigid stems.

Start seeds indoors in colder areas. Seeds sprout rapidly after the weather warms, and require only 6 to 8 weeks to grow to planting-out size. In warmer sections, sow seed directly in the open ground.

Like all dahlias, these bedding kinds perform best in moderate climates; where summers are hot, provide light afternoon shade.

Water regularly; remove faded blossoms to keep new flowers coming on.

Bedding dahlias' flowers in clear luminous colors are striking in arrangements — either alone or with fillers such as baby's breath. If you cut blossoms just before they are fully open, they will last at least 4 or 5 days.

Varieties: Unwin's Dwarf, with semi-double 3-inch flowers in a wide range of colors, is generally considered the best mixture. Coltness Hybrids have single flowers, some with fluted rays, in many colors.

Dahlia (dwarf Unwin)
(See color photograph on page 30)

DIANTHUS

(pinks)

Dianthus plants form mounds of gray-green, grass-like leaves. Slender 12 to 16-inch stems bear solitary loose clusters of several blossoms in shades of pink, red, rose, and white. Many—but not all—have a clove-like fragrance. Generally blooming in late spring or early summer, dianthus look best in drifts in old-fashioned borders among blue or white flowers: Chinese delphinium, forget-me-not, cynoglossum, or sweet alyssum. Dianthus also makes an excellent edging.

Annual dianthus grows quickly from seeds sown in full sun outdoors in fall or early spring. It is easy to start indoors and transplants easily. Dianthus tolerates almost any climate. Being frost-resistant it serves as a winter annual in areas where summers are too hot for it.

Pinks make charming bouquets when used alone, with their own clean foliage as filler. Or, try them in old-fashioned arrangements with flower spikes of English lavender, baby's breath, or candytuft.

Species and varieties: 'Bravo' (All-America) has deep scarlet red 1½-inch-wide blossoms on 8-inch-high plants. Excellent for edging white or blue flower beds.

Carnation-flowered types have fully double flowers like small carnations in shades of red, crimson, white and pink; grow to 1½ feet high.

'Gaiety' has large single blossoms with deeply cut, fringed, and slightly ruffled petals in unusual combinations of pink, deep red and white.

D. heddensis, a tetraploid hybrid, grows to 1½ feet tall, is vigorous, and heat resistant. The single blossoms are less frilled than 'Gaiety' but slightly larger, and borne in great quantities. Mixed colors.

Sweet William *(Dianthus barbatus),* although not an annual like the pinks, should be mentioned here. It's a biennial that flowers the second year. Nevertheless, the dwarf edging varieties (8 to 10 inches) are now being sold in nurseries in flats ready to flower and gardeners are using them like annuals. The fragrant flowers, in rounded clusters, are in similar colors to those of the pinks. The foliage is less grass-like and usually a rich green. You can also get the common sweet William that will grow 1 to 2 feet high. It grows easily from seed and usually self sows in the garden.

Some nurseries carry sweet William in separate colors: 'Giant White' carries large trusses of white flowers on 1½ to 2-foot stems; 'Newport Pink' is salmon pink. There also is a red variety.

WILLIAM APLIN

Dianthus 'Gaiety'
(Dianthus 'Bravo' (All-America)
is pictured in color on page 31)

FAIRY PRIMROSE

PRIMULA MALACOIDES

In gardens where frosts are rare, fairy primrose is a mainstay for winter and early spring bloom in part shade. In cold-winter areas it is sometimes grown in greenhouses. Dainty flowers in pink, white, rose, lavender, and crimson are borne in tiers on slender 12-inch-high stems above basal leaf rosettes.

Fairy primrose

In August, sow seeds in shallow furrows in flats of soil covered with ½ inch of vermiculite or sand. Cover seeds no more than ⅛ inch deep. Set flats in water and let them soak up all they will absorb, then cover with plastic sheeting and place in a shady spot. Water once a week until seeds sprout, then remove plastic. When seedlings have 4 leaves, transplant into shaded beds into which you have incorporated a 1-inch layer of peat moss or leaf mold. Keep soil moist and protect plants from drying winds.

Fairy primrose adds an airy grace to arrangements of spring flowering bulbs such as cyclamen, freesias, daffodils, Roman hyacinths, and smaller tulips. Blooms keep for several days.

Varieties: 'Tosca', crimson; 'Glory of Riverside', salmon pink; also available in white, lavender, and mixed colors.

FOUR O'CLOCK

MIRABILIS JALAPA (marvel of Peru)

When it comes to blooming, four o'clocks are truly late sleepers. Not only do they wait until midsummer to flower but—as their common name suggests—they also keep their flowers shut tight until late afternoon, unless the day is cloudy. Nevertheless, the plants' dense dark green foliage

Four o'clock

and profusion of trumpet-shaped red, yellow, pink, salmon, lavender, and white flowers act as refreshers in flower gardens that may be past their prime by fall. And they continue to bloom until frost blackens the foliage, usually in late October.

Actually, four o'clocks are perennials in mild-winter areas, but they are grown as annuals where winters are cold. Plants grow to 3 or 4 feet high in one summer, spreading to 3 feet. They make excellent temporary low hedges or screens, and they will quickly fill in tight, little-used areas.

Four o'clocks are especially popular in urban communities, because they are little affected by excess dust, fumes, and soot—simply wash them off with occasional light sprinkling.

Plants grow rapidly from the large seeds scattered in open, sunny, warm soil after frosts. Once you start four o'clocks, you're apt to find them coming up every summer, for they reseed readily.

Varieties: Available only in mixed colors. Flowers are often striped with contrasting colors.

FOXGLOVE

DIGITALIS PURPUREA

Although foxglove is a biennial, or sometimes a perennial, it will bloom in a year from seed started early the previous spring. This bold plant, with large woolly leaves in handsome rosettes, sends up 5 to 8-foot stalks topped with one-sided spike-like clusters of nodding, tubular, 3-inch flowers—white, pink, rose, or purple, dotted inside with darker colors.

To be sure of getting bloom the first year, start seeds of foxgloves indoors in early spring, transplant into small pots from which they may be set out in the garden. Where winters are severe, and there is no protective snow cover, mulch plants in late winter to keep frost from heaving the plants out of the ground.

Plant foxgloves in light shade where there is protection from wind. The plants re-seed readily; in some areas, cultivated foxgloves have gone wild and grow as freely as wild plants.

Varieties: Excelsior Hybrids have large white, pink, rose, purple, cream, and primrose yellow flowers arranged closely in a horizontal position all around the stem.

Shirley Hybrids have large bell-shaped blooms in shades of soft pink to deep rose, spotted with brown, maroon, or crimson.

JEANNETTE GROSSMAN
Foxglove

GAILLARDIA

G. PULCHELLA (annual gaillardia)

An easy-to-grow bedding plant that grows to 1½ to 2 feet high and has flower heads on long, whip-like stems during the summer months. Colors are warm shades of red, yellow, and gold. Flowers are excellent for cutting.

Plant seeds as you would zinnias or marigolds, in warm soil after frost danger is past.

Cut flowers keep for three or four days. Stems are weak, so the container should be selected accordingly. Some arrangers wire stems to hold them upright. Because of their flashy colors the flowers are best used by themselves, or with green foliage in copper bowls or other simple, plain-colored containers.

Varieties: G. *pulchella* 'Picta' is the usual garden form with large heads and succulent foliage. G. *p.* 'Lorenziana' has fluffier

Gaillardia

flower heads. Double Gaiety is a mixture that supplies flowers in many warm shades including some near-white and deep maroon.

GLOBE AMARANTH

GOMPHRENA GLOBOSA

These bushy-branched plants grow 2 to 3 feet high, and are covered with rounded clover-like flower heads ¾ inch wide. These may be magenta, purple, violet or white. Flower heads have the papery quality that classes them as an "everlasting."

This is an excellent plant for hot summer

Globe amaranth

areas. It is often grown as a companion for the annual Madagascar periwinkle.

In hot climates plant seeds (covered with a cottony lint) outdoors in warm soil as you would zinnias. Globe amaranth will grow well in northern states but the plants should be started indoors 8 to 10 weeks prior to frost-free date.

Fresh cut blossoms are useful in mixed bouquets. Flowers dry quickly and easily, retaining their color and shape for winter arrangements.

Varieties: Mixed colors are generally available. 'Buddy' (purple) and 'Cissy' (white) are dwarf edging varieties, not good for cutting.

GODETIA

G. AMOENA, often sold as G. GRANDIFLORA (satin flower, farewell-to-spring)

A cool-weather annual, 1 to 2½ feet high, which blooms in early summer. This western native is often grown with clarkia which also needs cool summers. It does well in New England, upper central states, and in high mountain areas. Flowers of the wild forms are pink, or lavender, to white above, pink or lavender at the base and either striped or blotched with red. Garden forms extend the range of color to salmon pink and pure white.

Sow seeds in place in late fall or early

Godetia

spring. Godetia prefers full sun except where summer days average over 80°.

Cut branches keep for several days in a cool room. Cut as soon as the top bud opens; others will open successively. For a pastel arrangement, combine salmon-pink godetia with Chinese delphinium, summer

forget-me-not, love-in-a-mist, or bachelor buttons.

Varieties: 'Sybil Sherwood', satiny salmon-pink flowers edged with white—an unusually fresh, lovely color.
'Kelvedon Glory', glowing salmon orange.
'White Swan', satiny white.

HOLLYHOCK

ALTHAEA ROSEA

Hollyhocks offer tall spires (to 7 feet high) of flowers in jewel-tone colors of crimson, pink, rose, salmon, scarlet, yellow, and also white. The large flowers may be single; semi-double; or frilly, fully double blooms like big pompoms.

In general, hollyhocks are biennial, producing only a basal clump of big kidney-shaped leaves the first year. However, seedsmen have developed annual strains that will flower the same year you plant the seeds.

Start seeds in peat pots indoors in late spring; transplant seedlings outdoors when danger of frost is past. Plants self sow readily.

Rust, a common disease on hollyhocks, can

Hollyhock (double)

be controlled by removing and destroying first leaves on which it appears; also by dusting with sulfur or spraying with Zineb as early in the attack as possible.

Varieties: Chater's Strain, from England, is offered by most American seedsmen. It supplies uniform plants almost all double flowered, in mixtures or single colors.

IMPATIENS

This genus includes three species. The plant known as balsam is the annual *I. balsamina*. Those commonly known as impatiens are *I. sultanii* and *I. holstii*. These are perennials that are often grown as annuals in cold-winter areas. Where winters are mild you may have them around for several years.

Balsam (*I. balsamina*). This old-time favorite is something of a stranger in today's gardens. Yet it has several virtues: Sturdy 8-inch to 2-foot plants are loaded with double flowers that look like miniature camellias, lasting for days on the plant, and dropping off when they begin to turn brown. Flower colors range from soft pink to rose pink, lilac, red, and white; some blooms have variegated colors. The mixed colors are most popular. The lower growing forms are useful for edgings, or you can grow them in pots to place on terraces or patios.

Balsam's fat seeds sprout in 4 to 5 days when planted in warm, moist soil outdoors. You can also start seeds indoors and set out transplants later. Balsam will grow in full sun except where summers are long and hot; in such areas, plant in light shade with protection from hot afternoon sun. Give them plenty of water and feed them about once a month; otherwise the plants will lose their glossy dark green color and look wilted. With good care plants bloom all summer long.

Balsam is not a good cut flower. Another common name—touch-me-not—comes from the fact that their seed capsules spring open and fling seeds far and wide when tapped sharply.

Impatiens. *I. holstii* and *I. sultanii* are similar in some respects, although *I. holstii* is taller (to 3 feet), more vigorous, with larger leaves and flowers. Both grow best in shade; both make good house plants. They have brittle, translucent stems and glossy foliage. The spurred blossoms in jewel-like colors of glowing orange or scarlet, crimson, rose, pink, and white, are borne in clusters held well above the foliage.

Start impatiens seeds indoors 10 to 12 weeks before warm weather. Use bottom heat of 70° to 75°. Plants are very tender

Impatiens balsamina

and will not tolerate frost or full sun.

Set 2 or 3 plants to a large pot, or arrange them in groups under trees. Impatiens needs frequent watering; spraying foliage with fine mist spray keeps plants clean and fresh. When plants have reached a good size, you can take cuttings, root them in sand, vermiculite, or water, and use them as indoor plants. They will bloom beautifully indoors except during the very short winter days.

Like balsam, it is not a good cut flower.

Varieties: The recently introduced dwarf varieties of *I. sultanii* from Europe grow to only 6 or 8 inches high and spread to 2 feet across. Flowers are about 1 inch wide and come in the usual impatiens colors—either solid or in mixtures.

KOCHIA

K. SCOPARIA, sold as K. 'CHILDSII'
(summer cypress, Belvedere)

These are foliage plants, usually grown close together for screens or individually

Kochia 'Childsii'

for their gently rounded 3-foot-high columnar form. Branches are densely clothed with very narrow soft leaves, making the plants too thick to see through. The green color is pleasant, and the billowy form makes up for the lack of flower color.

Seed kochia in full sun, outdoors. Grows quickly, and can be sheared for formal hedging. Owners of new homes often use kochia for temporary shrubs until the weather is cool enough to set out woody plants. Kochia tolerates high heat, yet will perform well in short-summer areas.

One variety, called Mexican fire bush (*K. scoparia* 'Culta', often sold under the name *K. scoparia* 'Trichophylla' as well as *K.* 'Childsii'), turns red with the first frost. It is an unkempt plant and reseeds so profusely that it quickly becomes a pest.

Larkspur
(See color photograph on page 30)

LARKSPUR

DELPHINIUM AJACIS

Larkspurs offer tall full spikes of 1 to 1½-inch-wide, spurred flowers in beautiful shades of blue, violet, rose, pink, and white, the blossoms often double. Plants may vary from 1 to 3 or 4 feet in height depending on the kind. They will bloom for about 2 months in late spring or early summer, then plants dry up.

Use larkspur as a background flower or in

front of a tall fence covered with sweet peas. Plant a solid edging of godetias, cynoglossum, or annual candytuft around larkspur beds to hide the low foliage which browns and mildews in early summer in cool, foggy areas.

Plant seeds in late summer where winters are mild. Seedlings are quite hardy. Scatter seeds over roughly prepared beds and water thoroughly—the washing action will cover seeds sufficiently. Where winters are severe, sow seeds in very early spring, no later than mid-April. Seedlings can be transplanted successfully when quite small.

Larkspur is a valuable cut flower that can be arranged in masses of single colors or in harmonizing shades such as soft pink to rose, or light blue to purple; pure white is stunning used alone. The blooms will keep for 3 or 4 days. Spikes can be dried successfully and will retain their color surprisingly well.

Varieties: In the Giant Imperial class are 'Blue Spire', dark blue; 'Brilliant Rose', 'Rosalie', and 'White King' (All-America). Mixed colors include carmine, cerise, and lavender shades, very dark blues, and all shades of pink.

LINARIA

L. MAROCCANA (toadflax)

Dainty, fast blooming, cool weather plants that grow to 10 to 15 inches high. Flowers faintly resemble a miniature snapdragon. In full bloom you can hardly see the leaves for the many spikes of fragile varicolored spurred blossoms. The colors are soft and unobtrusive—in white, lavender, violet, pink, purple, red, yellow, and chamois—so plant linaria in extensive drifts to show them up properly. Don't expect it to stay in bloom past July except in cool coastal areas and high mountain communities. Utilize its "instant bloom" to color up the fading foliage in tulip or daffodil beds, to brighten

Linaria

meadows or lanes, or to fill in among chrysanthemums while they are growing and setting buds.

Seed linaria in fall or very early spring. Plants stay in bloom longer if thinned to 1 foot apart. Prefers full sun but it develops in early summer before deciduous trees leaf out and can be planted under the fringes of boughs.

Varieties: Fairy Bouquet (All-America), 10 to 12 inches, is a mixture of pastel shades. Northern Lights, 12 to 15 inches, comes in mixed colors only—shades of lavender, violet, pink, purple, red, yellow, and white, marked and bicolored.

LOBELIA

(see page 36)

Madagascar periwinkle

MADAGASCAR PERIWINKLE

CATHARANTHUS ROSEUS, usually sold as VINCA ROSEA

In areas where there is sufficient summer heat, Madagascar periwinkle can be relied upon to produce abundant bloom long after zinnias and dwarf marigolds have burned out. It's a sturdy-stemmed, bushy plant that grows 1 to 2 feet high. Leaves are attractive—dark green and glossy. The 1 to 1½-inch-wide flowers, 2 to 3 in a cluster, are rose, white, or pink, some with a darker or contrasting eye.

Madagascar periwinkle grows slowly, so start seeds indoors except where summers are long and hot. Place seeded planter in a plastic bag; seeds will sprout in 7 to 10 days if temperatures are held at 70° to 75°. Plant seedlings in full sun in cool summer

areas, in part shade where summers are long and heat intense. Space them 6 inches apart to form solid beds. They also make good pot plants. Madagascar periwinkle is actually a short-lived perennial, so in areas where winters are exceptionally mild, the plants may live for more than one year.

Keep soil moist, but don't overwater or plants become spindly. Feed occasionally to keep foliage crisp and dark green. Madagascar periwinkle is relatively pest-free.

Flowers are rarely cut for arrangements.

Varieties: New, upright, 12-inch-high dwarf forms are the best: 'Bright Eye', white with red center; 'Little Pinkie', rose pink. 'Rose Carpet' grows only to 6 inches high. A good color mixture (2-foot-high plants) is also available.

MARIGOLD

TAGETES (see page 37)

MIGNONETTE

RESEDA ODORATA

Mignonette is not colorful enough to be a display flower, but its distinctive, sweet, clean fragrance is pleasant in the garden. Plants grow 12 to 18 inches high, and are rather sprawling. Foliage is light green. Small bronze and white flowers are in compact spike-like clusters; they dry up as soon as weather is hot.

Sow seeds in warm soil outdoors. Mignonette grows quickly and although it prefers

Mignonette 'Red Goliath'

full sun, it will take part shade. You can be assured of fragrance throughout the garden if you plant it in little patches here and there — among other annuals, near shrubs, by the doorstep, near a window you open frequently.

Bring the fragrance indoors by massing cut stems in a pottery bowl or bean pot. The cut blooms last for a week or more.

Varieties: 'Common Sweet Scented' or 'Machet' are preferred over the larger flowered but less fragrant 'Red Goliath'.

MIMULUS

(monkey flower)

Plants sold under the name of *M. tigrinus* are hybrids of *M. luteus*, its varieties, and *M. guttatus*. They are exceptionally large flowers — 2 to 2½ inches across on 6 to 12-inch-high plants. Blooms are brilliantly colored in red, yellow or gold, and strikingly marked, mottled, and variegated with brown or maroon.

Mimulus is rather touchy about its cultural requirements — cool, moist soil, and protection from direct sunlight (but not heavy shade). It will thrive in a woodsy spot where

Mimulus

moisture-loving plants such as ferns, violets, or bleeding heart are growing satisfactorily. Otherwise, grow it as a pot plant. Start seeds indoors in January or February to get good sized plants for 8-inch pots ready to plunge in beds outdoors after frost danger is past. Plants will need frequent feeding and watering to stay healthy in pots, but in the fall you can lift the pots and take plants indoors for winter bloom.

Cut flowers will last for 3 or 4 days in a cool room. Combine with fern fronds, primrose foliage, or with its own leaves.

'Queen's Prize' is a choice mixture of colors.

Dwarf morning glory

MORNING GLORY, DWARF

CONVOLVULUS TRICOLOR

These seldom-grown plants are gaining in popularity as pot plants and for hanging baskets. They are low-growing, trailing plants that grow to a foot high but spread to 2 or more feet. Display them on a low trellis or at the top of a wall where they can trail over.

Seed coats are tough and should be nicked with a file or punctured with a pin point. Seedlings are difficult to transplant and thus should be sown in place. They require full sun and considerable warmth. Dwarf morning glories are poorly suited to gardens where nights are cool. Keep plants on the dry side to encourage abundant bloom.

'Royal Ensign' spreads to 12 to 18 inches and has small 1½-inch-wide blossoms, bright blue with a yellow throat and white markings.

MORNING GLORY VINE

IPOMOEA PURPUREA

There's an exuberance about morning glory vines that makes you want to plant them where you can watch them grow and flower. The attractive foliage (large heart-shaped leaves) is dense enough to provide a temporary privacy screen. And you'll enjoy seeing the fresh display of large flowers opening daily — in shades of blue, white, pink, magenta, or crimson — all summer long.

To hasten germination of the hard seeds, nick the corner with a file. Plant them in full sun outdoors, or start in peat pots indoors and transplant them when the frost

danger is past. Keep plants moist, but do not overwater or overfeed or you'll get more foliage than flowers.

These vines require training to lead them up to fence tops, on trellises, or walls. Use sturdy string, wire, or light rope netting.

For arrangements, pick stems with flowers and buds in different stages of development. Place them in a deep vase and allow the vine-like stems to trail over the edge.

Varieties: 'Heavenly Blue' ranks as a top favorite; it is a deep blue, shading to cream in the center. 'Pearly Gates' (All-America) is pure white. 'Flying Saucers' comes in white and clear blue, in striped and mottled patterns. Morning glories also come in mixed colors: blue, white, pink, magenta, and crimson. Be sure to specify whether you want a large-flowered or small-flowered mixture.

DARROW M. WATT

Morning glory 'Flying Saucers'
('Heavenly Blue' in color on page 31)

NASTURTIUM

TROPAEOLUM MAJUS (see page 40)

NEMESIA

N. STRUMOSA

NEMESIA *N. strumosa*
A small bushy plant, about 8 inches tall, much used for early summer color in areas where days and nights are cool. The small orchid-like blossoms are borne in clusters in shades of pink, rose, orange, scarlet, blue, and yellow, marked in contrasting colors. Masses of nemesia edged with blue violas provide dazzling color. It's also attractive when interplanted in pots or patio containers.

Where winters are mild, plant nemesia out-

Nemesia

DARROW M. WATT

doors in full sun in fall or very early spring. A little protection from afternoon sun will extend the bloom period. Elsewhere plant outdoors in full sun after frost danger is past. When plants are 6 inches high, pinch off the tips of the tallest branches to get more compact plants. Keep soil moist (but not soggy); apply fertilizer regularly for abundant bloom.

Use these dainty blossoms in fairly dense bouquets in small-scale arrangements. Flowers will last for 2 or 3 days.

Varieties: 'Triumph' is a good blend of rich colors. Separate colors are available only from specialty seed houses or from England.

NICOTIANA

N. ALATA (flowering tobacco)

The sweet fragrance of nicotiana is especially provocative during the early evening hours in summer. Ample loose clusters bear large trumpet-shaped flowers in white, lav-

Nicotiana 'Sensation'

ender, mauve, crimson or maroon. Plants grow 2 to 3 feet high, and have large, coarse, velvety hairy leaves, especially near the base.

Nicotiana looks best in groups of 4 to 6 plants. Use them as upright accents among lower growing summer blooming flowers. Plant seeds in warm soil outdoors. The tiny seeds should not be covered with soil. Where summers are short, start seeds indoors as seeds sprout slowly. Once seeds are sprouted, plants develop rapidly. Nicotiana tolerates considerable heat if given some shade and in cooler areas will thrive in either full sun or semi-shade. It will flower from midsummer on, and plants self-sow readily.

Cut flowers last for 3 or 4 days — new blossoms open daily to replace yesterday's. Remove faded blossoms each day. Use nicotiana in old-fashioned bouquets. Cut whole stems in full bloom and place in deep water.

Varieties: The flowers of *N. alata* 'Grandiflora' open in the evening. The 2 to 3-foot-high plants come in the usual nicotiana colors, with white being the most fragrant. There are now varieties that open during daylight hours that are replacing the older Grandiflora mixture. They are lower growing (1½ to 2 feet high) and more compact. 'Sensation' comes in a good mixture including crimson, rose, lavender, cream, coral, and white. 'Daylight' is a good, fragrant dwarf white, 'Crimson Bedder' is also low growing, but less fragrant.

NIGELLA

N. DAMASCENA (love-in-a-mist)

Nigella is enjoying a comeback now that flower arrangers are using its dried seed capsules that are shaped like a small egg covered with bristles and branched spines (hence another common name, "devil-in-a-bush"). Plants grow to 18 inches high and are very fine and lacy in appearance. The

Nigella

1 to 1½-inch flowers are sky blue, sometimes white, and surrounded by a misty, lacy, green collar. These plants look best among other taller and more "solid" appearing annuals.

In fall or early spring sow seeds in full sun where plants are to remain. Plants come into bloom quickly and begin to dry up in late summer. Flower season can be somewhat prolonged with regular watering.

The lacy-fringed blue flowers add lightness and grace to bouquets of spring flowering bulbs. They are also effective with godetia, blue lace flower, sweet peas, snapdragons, and with their own foliage.

'Miss Jekyll', cornflower blue, is an excellent variety.

PANSY

VIOLA TRICOLOR HORTENSIS (see page 42)

PETUNIA

P. HYBRIDA (see page 44)

Annual phlox
(See color photograph on page 30)

PHLOX, ANNUAL

P. DRUMMONDII (pride of Texas)

This colorful 1 to 1½-foot-high annual provides ample flat clusters of 1-inch blossoms held well above the foliage. Flowers are rose, crimson, scarlet, white, salmon, soft pink, chamois, and violet, often with contrasting eyes. They are available in mixed and separate colors; some have frilled flowers; others are dwarf forms.

Sow phlox seed outdoors during cool weather, in either fall or spring. It germinates well in cool soil and quickly develops bushy plants. Or you can start seeds indoors; seedlings transplant easily. Where summers are cool, phlox blooms until early fall, but where summers are long and hot it is used as a spring flower to fill in between young plants of zinnias, tall marigolds, or cleome. Dwarf types make neat edgings or solid, brilliant beds.

Phlox is attractive in arrangements for 2 to 3 days if you pick off individual flowers as they shrivel. Mass by themselves, or combine with other flowers such as marigolds and zinnias in harmonious colors.

Varieties: 'Beauty' is the best color mixture. 'Twinkle' (All-America) supplies low growing compact plants with star-shaped blossoms. 'Glamour' (All-America), a tetraploid, has warm salmon colored flowers with centers a deeper shade.

PINCUSHION FLOWER

SCABIOSA ATROPURPUREA (sweet scabious, mourning bride)

Long slim stems are topped by compact rounded clusters of small flowers in lavender, lavender-blue, maroon, salmon pink, white, deep rose, deep mahogany, purple, and crimson. Bristling with stamens, the flower heads look like pincushions. These 3-foot-high plants bloom in early summer. Scabiosa thrives in most areas except those that are extremely hot, and they are easy to grow. Sow seeds in warm soil outdoors where plants are to remain. Keep plants closely spaced so that they will support each other — they will look less spindly, and the heavy blossom heads will be less apt to droop on their long wiry stems. Pinching off tip branches will also encourage bushier growth. Remove flowers as they fade.

Blossoms keep for several days after being

Pincushion flower

cut. Combine them with flowers of contrasting form such as annual phlox, or baby's breath.

Varieties: 'Heavenly Blue' (All-America), compact 18-inch-high plants with clear, lavender-like flowers. 'Black Night', tall, reddish black. 'Fire King', tall, scarlet. 'Peach Blossom', tall, pink. You can also get them in mixed colors.

Shirley poppy
(Iceland poppy is pictured in color on page 31)

POPPY

PAPAVER

Two poppies provide brilliant color in winter and spring or early summer. Both have large cup-shaped flowers with crinkly silken petals.

Shirley poppy (strains of corn poppy *P. rhoeas*) is an annual that bears its flowers on slender 2-foot-high stems in spring or early summer in cool regions. Many blossoms open in a short time from pendulous fat buds. Flower colors are in shades of pink, rose, white, salmon, and scarlet; some are double. You can buy them in mixtures. Two solid-color varieties are: 'Sweet Briar', deep rose-pink, double; 'American Legion', large, scarlet, single flowers with black cross inside cup.

Iceland poppy (*P. nudicaule*) is truly a perennial but is grown as an annual for winter bloom. Flower stems grow to 18 inches high, are somewhat more substantial than Shirley poppies and bloom over a longer period. Colors are in shades of white, orange, yellow, pink, and scarlet. The Gartford Giants offer large double flowers in mixed shades with wavy crinkled petals. Im-

perial Jewels have frilled and fluted petals in rich color blends.

Poppies are best planted in masses so that you'll always have fresh color coming to replace the short-lived blossoms. Their foliage is in basal rosettes.

Poppy seeds sprout quickly in cool soil; scatter in fall or spring. Iceland poppies can be started indoors where winters are severe and transplanted outdoors for early summer bloom. Their young leaves are extremely attractive to birds; cover the small plants with wire or cloth netting. Shirley poppy seed should be sown in place as they are not easily transplanted.

Cut poppies when buds first show color. Shirley poppies last for 2 or 3 days; Iceland poppy is not as dependable. Dip ends of cut stems in boiling water, or sear for a few seconds to seal in juices. Then place in deep cold water. Arrange in a vase that will hold several inches of water.

PORTULACA

P. GRANDIFLORA (rose moss)

Where you want exceptionally brilliant summer color for a temporary ground cover, in a sunny rock garden, or along a driveway strip, try portulaca. Flowers look like single or double small roses depending on the seed mixture you select. These mixtures provide clear colors of unusual lustre — vivid scarlet, yellow, pink, rose, salmon, orange, lavender, and white. Plants grow to only 6 inches high but will spread to 18 inches. Leaves are small, fleshy, and succulent.

Portulaca takes extreme heat and dryness of desert summers and does just as well where summers are short and cool.

In most areas start seeds indoors 2 months before average date of last frost. Place flat in a warm spot (70 to 75°) and seeds will germinate in 7 to 10 days. Where summers are long and hot, sow outdoors when soil is quite warm and keep beds moist until seeds sprout.

Portulaca

SALPIGLOSSIS

S. SINUATA (painted tongue)

The velvety petunia-like flowers of salpiglossis are richly colored in shades of mahogany red, red-orange, purple, and bicolors, with marbling and pencilings in gold or contrasting colors like a tapestry. They bloom lavishly from summer to first frosts. Plants are upright and open, grow 2 to 3 feet high. Use them as a background behind other cool-summer annuals such as nemesia, clarkia, or linaria.

Salpiglossis is not easy to grow. Seeds are quite fine, and plants can't take hot, humid weather. However, a well grown bed of salpiglossis is so outstanding that it's worth a try. Sow seeds in warm soil where plants are to remain. Scatter over soil which has been deeply watered then later worked into a fine texture. Lay old burlap over the seeded area and peg it down. Moisten it

Salpiglossis
(See color photograph on page 30)

with a gentle spray each evening. Seeds should sprout in 7 to 10 days. Remove burlap and water plants very sparingly as they grow.

Where summers are hot you can get large plants to set out early if you plant 6 seeds in a peat pot full of a good potting mixture. Later, thin to one plant.

Salpiglossis sprays keep for 3 or 4 days after cutting. Mass the colorful flowers in big copper or pottery bowls.

Varieties: 'Emperor', mixed colors, 3 feet tall. 'Bolero', an F-2, is shorter (2 to 2½ feet) and bushier, also in mixed colors.

SCARLET RUNNER BEAN VINE

PHASEOLUS COCCINEUS

This fast-growing annual vine has the happy property of producing both colorful flowers and beans that are edible when

Scarlet runner bean vine

young and green. Although basically a vegetable, this pole bean carries sprays of bright scarlet, sweet-pea shaped blossoms so attractive that it is often used for screening and for covering fences.

Sow the seeds in spring after frosts. The seeds are quite large, purple and black mottled; they germinate in about 4 days in warm soil. Vines climb to 6 to 10 feet by midsummer; like sunflowers and nasturtiums, they're good plants for children to grow.

Scarlet runner beans are subject to the usual garden pests; spray or dust with multi-purpose insecticide.

Pods are dark green, long and flattened. They should be eaten when about 4 inches long, as they become tough and fibrous with age.

SCARLET SAGE

SALVIA SPLENDENS (see page 48)

SNAPDRAGON

ANTIRRHINUM MAJUS (see page 49)

SNOW-ON-THE-MOUNTAIN

EUPHORBIA MARGINATA

This 2 to 3-foot-high plant is useful for its foliage rather than its flowers; the leaves are margined with white and the upper leaves surrounding the inconspicuous flowers are almost pure white. Use sparingly to blend diverse colors in perennial borders or to tone down hot colors such as orange or scarlet. Easy to grow, self sows readily, may become a weed unless thinned yearly. Sow seeds outdoors in warm soil in full sun. Seeds sprout rapidly and plants grow rapidly. They begin to develop the characteristic white edged leaves when only half grown.

Snow-on-the-mountain

Branches cut for foliage keep for several days if stem ends are dipped in boiling water or seared to congeal the milky juice. Use care in handling stems since the milky juice may cause a skin irritation. Foliage is attractive by itself or in combination with flowers such as white Shasta daisies, yellow marigolds or yellow, pink or white zinnias.

STATICE

LIMONIUM

For gardeners who like dried flower arrangements, this plant is an excellent source. Flowers are borne in open clusters of short one-sided spikes in late summer. The long 2-foot-high wiry stems are winged and arise from a dense clump of basal leaves. The flower calyx provides the color —blue, rose, purple, and yellow; tiny petals are creamy white. Their color lasts for an entire season in arrangements.

Sow seeds in full sun where plants are to remain. They have long taproots and do not transplant well. Statice needs good drainage; in fact, it does best when kept on the dry side. In areas where the summer season is especially rainy, or if given too much water, plants are subject to root rot.

Varieties: Gardeners usually plant mixed color seeds of statice, but single colors are available from specialty seed houses.

Statice

STOCK

MATHIOLA INCANA (see page 52)

STRAWFLOWER

HELICHRYSUM BRACTEATUM

One of the best everlastings, with glistening 2½-inch-wide pompon-like heads with colorful papery, petal-like bracts in yellow, orange, red, or white. Sturdy 2 to 3-foot-high plants have numerous long stems especially useful for cutting. Although strawflowers can be used in borders, they are too coarse to be featured up front.

Strawflower

Strawflowers are easy to grow. Plant seeds in late spring or early summer just as you would zinnias or marigolds. These annuals need full sun and are adapted to all but extremely hot summer climates. They will grow successfully in dry soil.

The colorful flowers are good when fresh in arrangements. Or if you wish to dry them, cut flowers before the yellow centers (disc flowers) show. Strip off the leaves and bundle each color separately. Wrap bundles in a newspaper cone and hang them upside down in a dry, shady place.

Varieties: An excellent color mixture includes shades of yellow, gold, white, crimson, ruby, and pink. Now available is a dwarf strain which is earlier blooming than the taller growing strawflowers.

SUNFLOWER

HELIANTHUS ANNUUS

Sunflower is a "funflower." No other annual grows as tall, as fast, or as easily. Children thrill to the sight of a towering sunflower they grew from a seed even smaller than a bean. You can toast and eat the hundreds of delicious seeds in the huge heads, too, if songbirds don't beat you to them. (Crack them like nuts for the tasty "meat" inside.)

In cool, windy areas, the plants grow to about 6 feet; on the warm, sheltered side of a house or garage, they may reach 15 feet. Huge daisy-like single or double flowers are gold, red, bronze, or brown. Rough textured, dark green leaves are often 12 inches long.

Plant seed ½ inch deep in warm soil. Sunflower plants consume huge amounts of water. Let the hose trickle around growing plants for an hour or so twice a week. If you want extremely big sunflower stalks and heads, apply a complete fertilizer and a 2 or 3-inch mulch of compost.

To use as cut flowers, pick blooms when they are cup-size or smaller. Arrange them by themselves in big copper or pottery bowls.

Varieties: 'Mammoth' is very tall growing, and has blossoms 8 to 14 inches in diameter, with a single row of golden rays around a center of disk flowers; large seeds are gray-striped or black.

'Double Sungold' produces clusters of very double, 4 to 6-inch, golden, dahlia-like flowers with slightly quilled rays. The 4 to 6-foot plants are good for backgrounds or against high fences.

'Red and Gold' is a variety growing 4 to 6 feet tall. Flowers have long rays zoned with bands of red, maroon, deep brown, and yellow.

Sunflower

SWEET PEA

LATHYRUS ODORATUS (see page 53)

SWEET SULTAN

CENTAUREA MOSCHATA

Spreading plants with ascending branches, growing to 2 feet high. Leaves are deeply toothed and the 2-inch-wide yellow, lilac, purple, rose, or white thistle-like flowers have a musk-like fragrance.

Sweet sultan lacks the body and substance

Sweet sultan

for a good bedding plant. It is best used in drifts among other spring and early summer blooming plants such as white candytuft or cynoglossum.

Sow seed of sweet sultan in the fall in all areas except those where winters are long and severe. Even though you don't get around to seeding until January or February, you will get good bloom if you sow it in full sun, since plants grow very rapidly. Seed can be broadcast on the snow or simply scattered on roughly prepared beds; spring rains will cover the seeds. Calendula, viola, or pansy seedlings can replace sweet sultan after you pull them out in late summer.

SWEET WILLIAM

(see DIANTHUS)

TITHONIA

T. ROTUNDIFOLIA (Mexican sunflower)

Tithonia is one of the few flowers that will bloom gaily during August and September in spite of desert heat and extreme dryness. The daisy-like flowers are 3 to 4 inches wide with orange-scarlet rays and tufted yellow centers. Plants are robust, grow to 4 to 6 feet high and as wide. They are actually perennials 8 to 12 feet high in their native Mexico and Central America, but are usually grown as annuals in this country. Although the foliage is coarse and not attractive, the flaming flowers are so vivid you'll hardly notice the leaves. They are best used as backgrounds or informal temporary hedges in places where the color won't clash with other flowers.

Plant seeds in warm soil outdoors and thin seedlings to 4 feet apart. Allow plenty of room for plants to spread. In cold-winter areas plant seeds indoors in pots; by the time frost danger is past, you'll have 8 to 12-inch plants ready to set out that will bloom in August. In these areas, plants

Tithonia 'Torch' (All-America)

seeded directly in the ground won't bloom until September .

When gathering flowers for arrangements, handle stems carefully as flowers break off easily. Like sunflowers, marigolds, and zinnias, they arrange most effectively by themselves in abundant masses in big bowls. To add a light touch, use baby's breath or statice as a filler.

Varieties: 'Torch' (All-America) grows to 4 feet.

TORENIA

T. FOURNIERI (wishbone flower)

This is a charming, little known, but worthwhile plant for summer and fall bloom in part shade. And it's easy to grow.

The bushy neat plants grow to 1 foot high and have bronzy green foliage. Gloxinia-like flowers — sky blue with violet lower lips and a yellow throat — are borne in profusion. There are also white flowered forms.

Torenia

Torenia grows well in all 50 states. Only where summers are cool and short should it be grown in full sun. Plant torenia in warm soil where it is to remain; its seeds won't sprout until the soil is quite warm. For earlier bloom, start seeds indoors; seedlings transplant easily. Plants like plenty of humidity; blossoms tend to fade quickly where the air is dry.

An informal planting of torenia on the fringes of a grove of trees is most attractive. Or try them in containers in half shade. Combine with edgings of lobelia or fibrous begonia, or with a background of ferns. In hanging baskets use it with trailing lobelia. Torenia blossoms are short lived in arrangements and are difficult to pick without damaging the plant.

VERBENA

V. HYBRIDA, usually sold as V. HORTENSIS

Although verbena is a perennial, it is grown as an annual in most parts of the country; where winters are mild it lives over, along with petunias and snapdragons.

Verbena

Many-branched plants reach 10 inches high and spread 1½ to 2 feet. Oblong, 2 to 4-inch leaves are bright green or gray-green, with toothed margins. Flowers are carried in flat compact clusters in shades ranging from light lavender-blue to intense deep violet, from lightest pink to red, and white and cream. Many flowers have contrasting centers. Blooms hold their color even in intense sunlight.

Sow seeds of verbena in warm soil outdoors; start them indoors where the summers are short. Seedlings are a little slow to start indoors and need warmth and ample light for good growth. In the garden, plants tolerate

high heat but require lots of water.

Verbena is often used as a cut flower; young, partially open clusters will hold for 2 or 3 days. Plants quickly grow new branches to replace those removed for bouquets.

Varieties: Verbena is available in giant, dwarf compact, tall erect, and dwarf erect forms. Rainbow Mixture, dwarf erect form 8 inches tall, blooms several weeks ahead of other kinds.

VIRGINIAN STOCK

MALCOLMIA MARITIMA

If you live in a cool-weather area and want a quick show of spring flowers, try Virginian stock. It blooms in 6 weeks after planting seed. Its only resemblance to garden stock is in its flower colors — cream, pink, white, rose, lavender, and magenta. It grows 6 to 8 inches high. Virginian stock effectively covers out-of-bloom bulb beds, rocky outcroppings, or "natural" meadows.

Sow seeds in early spring where plants are to remain. Full sun is preferred, but plants grow so fast that they will bloom under deciduous trees before they leaf out.

The faintly fragrant flowers in small clusters show off best in dense bouquets.

Virginian stock

VIOLA

VIOLA CORNUTA (see page 42)

ZINNIA

(see page 56)

PRONUNCIATION GUIDE

READING about annuals is one thing; conversing about them is another. Many of the botanical names are tongue-twisters.

This section should help you to talk about annuals with a new ease and confidence. Because accentuation is a primary stumbling block, syllables to be stressed are printed in capitals.

GENERA
(The first name)

Ageratum — Aj-er-RAY-tum
Althaea — AL-thee-uh
Alyssum — Al-LISS-um
Amaranthus — Am-ar-RANTH-us
Anagallis — An-ag-GAL-liss
Anchusa — An-KEW-suh
Antirrhinum — An-tihr-RYE-num
Artemisia — Art-em-MIZ-ee-uh
Browallia — Broh-WAL-lee-uh
Calendula — Kal-LEND-yew-luh
Calliopsis — Kal-lee-OP-siss
Callistephus — Kal-LISS-tef-us
Campanula — Kam-PAN-yew-luh
Catharanthus — Kayth-uh-RAN-thuss
Celosia — Sel-LOH-shee-uh
Centaurea — Sen-taw-REE-uh
Cineraria — Sin-er-RAY-ree-uh
Clarkia — KLARK-ee-uh
Cleome — Klee-OH-mee
Coleus — KOH-lee-us
Convolvulus — Kon-VOLV-yew-lus
Coreopsis — Koh-ree-OP-siss
Cosmos — KOZ-moss
Cynoglossum — Sin-oh-GLOSS-um
Dahlia — DAHL-yuh
Delphinium — Del-FIN-ee-um
Dianthus — Dye-ANTH-us
Didiscus — Dye-DISS-cuss
Digitalis — Dij-it-TAY-liss
Dimorphotheca — Dye-mor-foh-THEEK-uh
Eschscholzia — Esh-SHOLT-see-uh
Euphorbia — Yew-FORB-ee-uh
Gaillardia — Gay-LARD-ee-uh
Godetia — Goh-DEE-shee-uh
Gomphrena — Gom-FREE-nuh
Gypsophila — Jip-SOFF-il-uh
Helianthus — Hee-lee-ANTH-us
Helichrysum — Hel-ik-KRYE-sum
Iberis — Eye-BEER-iss
Impatiens — Im-PAY-shee-enz
Ipomoea — Eye-poh-MEE-uh
Kochia — KOH-kee-uh
Lathyrus — LATH-ihr-us
Limonium — Lim-MOH-nee-um
Linaria — Lye-NAY-ree-uh

Lobelia — Loh-BEEL-ee-uh
Malcolmia — Mal-KOH-mee-uh
Mathiola — Math-EYE-oh-luh
Mimulus — MIM-yew-lus
Mirabilis — Mihr-RAB-il-iss
Molucella — Mol-yew-SELL-uh
Nemesia — Nem-MEESH-ee-uh
Nemophila — Nee-MOFF-il-uh
Nicotiana — Nik-oh-shee-AY-nuh
Nigella — Nye-JELL-uh
Papaver — Pap-PAY-ver
Petunia — Pet-TEW-nee-uh
Phaseolus — Fas-SEE-ol-us
Phlox — FLOX
Portulaca — Port-yew-LAY-kuh
Primula — PRIM-yew-luh
Quamoclit — KWAM-oh-klit
Reseda — Res-SEED-uh
Salpiglossis — Sal-pig-GLOSS-iss
Salvia — SAL-vee-uh
Scabiosa — Skay-bee-OH-suh
Schizanthus — Skye-ZANTH-us
Sempervivum — Sem-per-VYE-vum
Senecio — Sen-NEE-see-oh
Statice — STAT-iss-ee
Tagetes — Taj-JEET-eez
Thunbergia — Thun-BERJ-ee-uh
Tithonia — Tith-OH-nee-uh
Torenia — Tor-REEN-ee-uh
Trachymene — Trak-KIM-en-ee
Tropaeolum — Trop-PEE-ol-um
Verbena — Ver-BEE-nuh
Vinca — VIN-kuh
Viola — VYE-ol-uh
Zinnia — ZINN-ee-uh

SPECIES, VARIETIES
(Second and/or third names)

ajacis — a-JAY-cus
alata — al-LAY-tuh
amabile — am-MAB-il-ee
amara — am-MAY-ruh
americana — am-eh-rik-KAY-nuh
amoena — am-MEEN-uh
angustifolia — an-gus-tif-FOH-lee-uh
annuus — AN-yew-us
argentea — ar-JEN-tee-uh
atropurpurea — at-roh-per-PEW-ree-uh
aurantiaca — aw-ran-TYE-ak-uh
balsamina — bal-SAY-meen-uh
barbatus — bar-BAY-tus
bipinnatus — bye-pin-NAY-tus
blumei — BLUE-mee-eye
bracteatum — brak-tee-AY-tum
caerulea — see-REW-lee-uh
californica — kal-if-FORN-ik-uh
calycanthema — kal-ee-KAN-them-uh
candidum — KAN-did-um
capensis — kap-PEN-siss
caudatus — kaw-DAY-tus
childsii — CHILD-zee-eye
chinensis — chin-NEN-siss

coccineus — kok-SIN-ee-us
cornuta — kor-NEW-tuh
cristata — kris-TAY-tuh
cruentus — krew-EN-tus
culta — CULT-uh
cyanus — sye-AY-nus
damascena — dam-ass-SEE-nuh
drummondii — drum-MON-dee-eye
elegans — ELL-eg-anz
fournieri — for-nee-AIR-eye
globosa — gloh-BOH-suh
grandiflora — gran-dif-FLOH-ruh
guttatus — gut-TAY-tus
haageana — HAG-ee-ay-nuh
heddensis — hed-DEN-sus
holstii — HOL-stee-eye
hortensis — hor-TEN-siss
houstonianum — hews-STONE-ee-ayn-um
hybrida — HIB-rid-uh
hybridus — HIB-rid-us
hypochondriacus — hypo-KON-dree-aye-cus
incana — in-KAY-nuh
insignis — in-SIG-niss
jalapa — juh-LAP-uh
laevis — LEE-viss
linifolia — lye-nif-FOH-lee-uh
lorenziana — lor-EN-zee-ayn-uh
majus — MAJ-us
malacoides — mal-ak-KOY-deez
margarita — mar-gar-RYE-tuh
maritima — mar-RIT-im-uh
maroccana — mar-rok-KAY-nuh
medium — MEE-dee-um
menziesii — men-ZEE-see-eye
merkii — MERK-ee-eye
moschata — mos-KAY-tuh
nudicaule — new-dik-KAWL
odorata — oh-dor-RAY-tuh
officinalis — off-iss-in-NAY-liss
picta — PIK-tuh
pinnatus — pin-NAY-tus
pulchella — pull-KELL-uh
pumila — PEW-mil-uh
purpurea — pur-PEW-ree-uh
rhoeas — REE-us
rosea — ROH-zee-uh
roseus — ROH-zee-us
rotundifolia — roh-tun-dif-FOH-lee-uh
scoparia — skop-PAY-ree-uh
sinuata — sin-yew-AY-tuh
sinuatum — sin-yew-AY-tum
sloteri — SLO-ter-eye
speciosa — spee-see-OH-suh
spinosa — spye-NOH-suh
splendens — SPLEN-denz
strumosa — strew-MOH-suh
sultanii — sul-TAN-ee-eye
tectorum — tek-TOHR-um
tigrinus — tig-RYE-nus
tinctoria — tink-TOH-ree-uh
trichophylla — trik-oh-FILL-uh
tricolor — TRYE-kol-or
umbellata — um-bel-LAY-tuh

INDEX